or return on

Business management (IYCB 3) Handbook

BUSINESS MANAGEMENT

(IYCB 3) HANDBOOK

Claes-Axel Andersson
Derek Miles
John Ward

International Labour Office   Geneva

Andersson, C. A., Miles, D., Ward, J.
Business management (Improve Your Construction Business 3) Handbook
Geneva, International Labour Office, 1996
/Management development/, /Guide/, /Management/, /Financial management/, /Construction/, /Small scale industry/, /Construction industry/. 12.04.1
ISBN 92-2-108755-7
ISBN for complete set of two volumes: 92-2-109314-X
ISSN 1020-0584

ILO Cataloguing in Publication Data

Printed in France   WEI/DAR

PREFACE

The *Improve Your Business (IYB)* approach to small enterprise development has proved its worth in many different countries, and has demonstrated the need for publications which are written simply and clearly but which can still communicate the basic management knowledge required by entrepreneurs if they are to run small businesses successfully.

Although all small businesses face some common problems and certain management principles are universal, experience has shown that a sector-specific development of the IYB approach would be widely welcomed.

This demand was particularly strong from enterprises in the construction sector, since small contractors have to cope with the special managerial problems that arise from bidding for and carrying out varied and dispersed projects and are faced with highly cyclical demand.

The ILO has responded by developing this Improve Your Construction Business (IYCB) series to suit the specific needs of small building and public works contractors. The IYCB series of three handbooks and workbooks is available either separately or as a set, and comprises:

Pricing and bidding (IYCB 1) – Handbook and Workbook
Site management (IYCB 2) – Handbook and Workbook
Business management (IYCB 3) – Handbook and Workbook

They have been designed for self-study, but there is also an IYCB trainer's guide to assist trainers in preparing for and running seminars and workshops. As demand emerges, further handbooks and workbooks will be added to suit the specialist needs of, for example, road contractors and materials manufacturers.

The first handbook and workbook cover pricing and bidding to obtain new projects. Too many contractors produce "guesstimates" – not estimates – of project costs, so they either bid too high and lose the contract or – often even worse – get the work at a price which is below cost. Besides taking the reader step-by-step through the preparation of the bid for a small building contract, the first handbook contains a contract glossary.

The second handbook and workbook start where the first set finishes – a potentially profitable contract has been won. The first part of these books, "planning for profit" helps the reader to prepare a realistic plan to carry out the work, while the second part "making it happen" deals with the principles and practice of site supervision.

The third handbook and workbook cover business management. A contracting firm is not just a collection of individual contracts; it is also a business enterprise. These books focus on financial control and office administration, which are frequently neglected by contractors who are generally more interested in the technical aspects of building work.

The way the IYCB system works is that the *handbook* provides ideas and information and the *workbook* gives the reader a chance to look at his or her business in a disciplined way, and decide on action plans to make it more competitive and successful. Together, the IYCB series should enable you, as the owner or manager of a small construction enterprise, to improve *your* construction business. As joint authors with between us about a hundred years' experience of working with small contractors around the world, we understand the risky and demanding environment in which you work and hope that the IYCB series will help you and your firm to survive and prosper.

This book was prepared and edited under the auspices of the ILO's Construction Management Programme, which was initiated within the Entrepreneurship and Management Development Branch of the Enterprise and Cooperative Development Department, and is now based in the Policies and Programmes for Development Branch of the Employment and Development Department.

Claes-Axel Andersson

Derek Miles

John Ward

THE AUTHORS

Claes-Axel Andersson manages the Improve Your Construction Business project within the ILO Construction Management Programme based in its Policies and Programmes for Development Branch. He is a professionally qualified civil engineer with extensive experience in project management and building design.

Derek Miles is Director of Overseas Activities in the Department of Civil Engineering of Loughborough University of Technology, United Kingdom, and was previously Project Coordinator of the ILO Construction Management Programme. He is a Fellow of the Institution of Civil Engineers and the British Institute of Management and has more than 20 years' experience in the development of national construction industries.

John Ward is an independent consultant specializing in training for construction enterprises, and was previously chief technical adviser to the first Improve Your Construction Business project. He started his career as site agent and engineer with major construction companies, then ran his own small contracting business before specializing in the training of owners and managers of small construction enterprises.

ACKNOWLEDGEMENTS

The *Improve Your Business (IYB)* approach to small enterprise development was conceived by the Swedish Employers' Confederation, and has since been developed internationally by the ILO with financial assistance from the Swedish International Development Authority (SIDA) and other donors.

The authors particularly wish to acknowledge the contribution of Kaarina Kalla, a training and information specialist and consultant to the ILO, who reviewed the sections of this handbook which deal with the financial aspects of business management.

The Government of the Netherlands agreed to finance the first "Improve Your Construction Business" (IYCB) project, based at the Management Development and Productivity Institute (MDPI) in Accra.

Ghana proved a good choice. As a result of recent changes there is a favourable climate for private sector initiatives, and Ghanaians have a well-deserved reputation for entrepreneurial drive. The Civil Engineering and Building Contractors Association of Ghana (CEBCAG) appreciated the opportunity that the project offered for its members to improve their management skills, and worked closely with the MDPI team and the ILO chief technical adviser to ensure that the training programme met the most urgent needs of its members.

This initial IYCB project provided an opportunity to develop and test a series of *Improve Your Construction Business* handbooks and workbooks and we wish to specifically acknowledge the dedication and enthusiasm of the MDPI/CEBCAG training teams or "cohorts".[1] The project package contained a certain amount of material that was specific to operating conditions in Ghana, but this published edition has been carefully edited to meet the general needs of small-scale construction entrepreneurs for basic advice on ways to improve business performance.

[1] Yahaya Abu, Michael Adjei, Margaret Agyemang, Kofitse Ahadzi, Henry Amoh-Mensa, Ernest Asare, John Asiedu, Franklin Badu, Fidelis Baku, Siegward Bakudie, Joseph Dick, Hamidu Haruna, Mathias Kudafa, D. Nsowah, Eric Ofori, Yaw Owusu-Kumih, S. Sakyi, Harry Seglah.

CONTENTS

Figures

Tables

HOW TO USE THIS HANDBOOK

This handbook is written for *you* – the owner or manager of a small construction business. Together the three basic IYCB handbooks provide advice on most aspects of running such a business, and the three complementary workbooks give you the chance to test your management skills, assess the performance of your business in a disciplined way and develop your own action plans.

Improve Your Construction Business is material for you to work with. It is available in a series of modules which take you step-by-step through the different stages of running a small contracting business. They are best read together. We suggest you first read the chapter in the handbook, and then work through the examples in the corresponding chapter of the workbook.

This handbook

This handbook is divided into two parts: A: Managing your money and B: Managing your business. In Part A, the first chapter will make you think about different ways of financing your business. The following four chapters are devoted to cash-flow calculations, demonstrating how to calculate a cash-flow forecast and showing what you can learn from such an analysis. The last three chapters in Part A give advice on how to bill your client for work done, and how to price equipment and material correctly. Part B starts by looking at how properly kept accounts can help you to manage your business better, and follows with three chapters giving advice on how to manage your office and workshop more efficiently. The last chapter introduces you to marketing which is a very important subject, unfortunately often neglected by contractors.

This handbook is both a basic textbook and a reference book, employing a step-by-step approach, designed to help you manage your company better. The chapters are set out in the same order as the chapters in the workbook, so that you can easily go from workbook to handbook or from handbook to workbook.

The workbook

The workbook enables you to test your skills by means of exercises in management practice. It will show you how to use specific tools, such as cash-flow forecasts and business accounts, to control and plan your own business as well as giving advice on how to manage your office and workshop better.

In each chapter of the Workbook there is a list of simple questions to which you answer "yes" or "no". The answers you write will tell you about the strengths and weaknesses of your business.

If you find that you need to improve your management skills in certain areas after going through the workbook, you can turn back to the appropriate section in the handbook and make sure you understand all the items and techniques introduced there.

Where to start

The following route map will help you to find your way around the handbook. We recommend that you start by reading quickly through the whole book. Then you can go back over it more slowly, concentrating on the chapters which deal with those parts of management which you think are weakest in your business.

Managing your money				Managing your business			
Financing your business	Cash-flow – Concepts Cash flow – Costs Cash flow – Income Cash flow – Analysis	Measurement and payment Materials purchase and control	Costing plant and equipment accounts	Book-keeping and company records	Office management and	Workshop management	Marketing
Describes how business finance is obtained and how it can be used, explains the importance of forecasting and controlling cash needs, how to get payment from clients for work done and how to control plant and materials costs.				Explains how to prepare and understand business accounts, how to manage your office, the importance of keeping proper company records, how to manage your workshop and how to obtain and keep clients and customers.			
Chapter 1	Chapter 2 Chapter 3 Chapter 4 Chapter 5	Chapter 6 Chapter 8	Chapter 7 Chapter 10	Chapter 9 Chapter 12	Chapter 11	Chapter 13	Chapter 14

As soon as you feel comfortable with the ideas in a particular chapter, you can try out your skills in the workbook. Together this handbook and workbook and the others in the IYCB series, should become your "business friends".

> Note: Since this book is intended for use in many different countries, we have used the term "NU" in the examples to represent an imaginary "National Unit of currency" and NS to stand for imaginary "National Standards".

PART A
MANAGING YOUR MONEY

FINANCING YOUR BUSINESS   I

Cars run on petrol or diesel fuel. Businesses run on money. A well-designed car gets you a long way on a small quantity of fuel. You should design your business so that you get the maximum return on your investment of capital. To achieve this, a considerable amount of time will have to be spent in analysing your business and making financial calculations. These activities are an essential part of your business plan. Few people who start a business have an in-depth understanding of accounting. Nevertheless, this is an area of starting and managing a business that cannot be ignored or left entirely to an accountant. Almost every business decision has a financial dimension. Since the first reason for small business failure is bad management and the second reason is problems in obtaining finance, then you need to develop competency in both these areas.

Where the money comes from

A good financial plan is a necessity for every enterprise. Financial analysis makes it possible to estimate how much money you need to run your business as well as to guarantee profit. Financial plans allow you to look before you leap. Good financial planning facilitates business growth and enables financial control. You need to understand the basic concepts in order to calculate the figures.

To avoid the second cause of small business failure, which is finance and especially lack of capital, you should carefully consider different sources of funding your business. These funds can be divided into:

❑ Equity capital

❑ Borrowed capital

❑ Retained profits.

Many entrepreneurs either fail to prepare an estimate at all, or they underestimate the amount of money needed to run their business. An accurate estimate should be made of how much capital will be needed to keep the business running. Do not cheat yourself or you will end up in trouble with creditors. The question to ask is: "Am I really using my capital and my profits wisely to develop my business?"

Liabilities

Businesses need capital because they have *liabilities*. Liabilities are obligations owed by the business to people who provide it with capital, goods or services. Even the capital you put into your own business is a liability as far as the business is concerned, because everything left over when all the debts are paid must always belong to its owners. This explains why balance sheets "balance", in that total assets must always equal the total liabilities.

Funds will be needed for both working capital and fixed capital/fixed assets. Working capital is the excess of current assets over current liabilities. You might think of the working capital as money that pays for the immediate costs of running the business until payments come in from the client. Fixed assets, such as the plant and equipment needed to earn the profit on a long-term basis, represent a more permanent investment in the business and can only be repaid gradually out of profits. The amount of working capital required and the need for fixed assets can both be calculated in advance, so that the cost of carrying out a contract is known.

EQUITY CAPITAL

Your own money

The owners of a business always have to bear the first share of the risk. You should calculate how much of your own money you are able to invest in the business, but you must also decide after every successful year how much of the profit you should retain for future investment. If you do not have enough assets of your own to finance your business, it might be worth thinking about going into partnership. Partnerships consist of two or more people who go into business as joint owners. It is often the case that one person has the construction skills and the other has capital and some knowledge of accounting and business practices.

Other people's money

If you manage to convince your friends or relatives of the probable future success of your business they might be prepared to put up long-term capital in return for a share in the profits. Alternatively you could think about going into partnership with someone who has sufficient capital, and who may also bring useful commercial skills into your business.

BORROWED CAPITAL

Loans

If you do not have enough capital of your own and you do not have access to mobilization advances (see section below), you will either have to get a loan from a bank or look for some other source of outside capital. Bank loans can be very useful for a growing business, but it is dangerous to rely too heavily on bank loans and overdrafts because they are essentially short- or medium-term capital, and the bank usually reserves the right to ask for repayment with very little notice. This could be a real problem if your money is tied up in plant and materials and your clients delay payment for some reason. It is very difficult for a small business to negotiate long-term loans, although development banks are sometimes prepared to help in this way. The best way to build healthy finances is to run your business efficiently and plough back profits instead of borrowing from others.

Loans from individuals

It is certainly attractive to run your business on other people's money, usually in the form of a loan that has to be repaid out of profits in the short or medium term. Money can even be seen as a resource, like labour, materials or equipment, which you hire in order to complete your projects. But borrowing money is expensive, and the lender will require a high interest if your business might be risky.

Bank loans and overdrafts

Banks are prepared to make loans to cover the need for working capital or fixed assets, but they are a source of temporary rather than permanent borrowing. Unfortunately the construction industry has a poor reputation with many banks, so you need to prepare carefully before visiting a bank manager to ask for a loan.

The bank manager will want to check your reputation by taking references from your clients or your suppliers. Banks are businesses, and like other businesses they need to make profits and avoid losses. The money that they lend is borrowed from other people's savings. Thus it is the job of the bank manager to make sure that money is only lent to people who can be relied on to make repayments strictly in accordance with their commitments.

Business books and accounts for

borrowed money

The first things that the bank manager will want to see are your business books and accounts.

These are important for two reasons:

❑ they show whether your business is sound and in good health;

❑ the way you keep your books will tell an experienced bank manager or accountant whether you are in control of the financial side of your business or not.

If you do not think your business will pass these two basic tests, you will almost certainly be wasting your time even thinking about asking for a loan. If you do believe your business will pass the tests, then you need to work out exactly how much cash you need to borrow and when you will be able to pay it back. If you are able to prepare accurate, reliable calculations, your chances of convincing the bank manager are much greater.

No business can succeed without clients or customers. So if you are a manufacturer of building materials or a jobbing builder, you need to produce evidence that there is a real demand for the product or service that you offer. If you are a contractor seeking a loan or overdraft for working capital, the bank manager will want to see proof that you have been awarded a contract. Rough ideas about cash needs are not good enough. The money that is borrowed will have to be paid back, with interest, during a specified period. It is your job to show the bank manager that you are able to do this. This means that you have to calculate – rather than guess – the amount you need to borrow.

Collateral

Even if your cash-flow calculations are convincing, the bank will want a guarantee that it will get its money back if your business does not perform as well as you expect. The bank safeguards its position by asking for collateral, which means some form of asset that could be sold to repay the loan if your business fails. Collateral generally takes the form of property or land, but it could be anything else of value that you own – providing it can easily be sold in an emergency. The market value of the collateral must be at least equal to the amount of the loan, but most banks will approve only part of its value, maybe 60 per cent, since in many cases it may be difficult to sell your property within a short time.

MOBILIZATION ADVANCES

In some countries where the government is actively encouraging small contractors, it is possible to get a "mobilization advance", which is really a short-term loan from the client, if you win a government contract. The client will advance up to about one-third of the amount of the contract to help you start up.

The client will require some collateral or other evidence of security and will not actually give you the money outright, but will pay for materials or equipment bought for the contract. The client recovers the loan in monthly instalments from the money you earn on the contract. All the money will have to be repaid before the contract is completed.

RETAINED PROFITS

The best and safest way of expanding your business is out of retained profits. When you make a profit, it is always tempting to go on a spending spree, to impress your neighbours, to show you are making some money.

❏ Resist this temptation.

❏ Use the profit to improve your business.

❏ Money invested wisely now will ensure a more prosperous future (ploughing back the profits).

In the next chapters of this handbook we will help you to improve your cash management. You should remember the difference between profit and cash, never confuse these two concepts. You need the profit from good estimating (Handbook 1) and good site management (Handbook 2) to survive in the long term. But you also need good cash management to keep your working capital moving and growing, otherwise your business will not survive long enough for you to achieve that profit.

How to use your money wisely

FIXED ASSETS AND WORKING CAPITAL

This handbook helps you to calculate your need for fixed assets and working capital. Both are important, and you need enough of both if your business is to survive.

Fixed assets

Fixed assets have a relatively long life (more than one year), are permanent in nature and are used by the business in its operations. Fixed assets are such items as land and buildings, plant and machinery, and can include vehicles, batching plant, concrete mixers and dumpers. You need to limit the amount you tie up in fixed assets, so that you have enough working capital to run your other business activities. Permanent premises, such as offices and a yard, may be unnecessary for the small contractor who can generally use each site as a yard.

Working capital

Working capital is the money that is circulating around your business in the same way that blood circulates around your body. If you do not have enough of it, your business will die. The general rule is that you always need a little more working capital than you expect, because costs tend to increase and clients are often slow to settle their accounts. Worse still, if the rumour goes round that your business is short of cash, your workforce will ask for advances on wages, and materials suppliers and subcontractors will no longer offer credit. In general, the greater the working capital the more stable is your business.

You need money for investments, for hiring or leasing machinery, for paying labour costs, interest, rents and so on – in other words to run your business. The first decision is whether to buy or hire the plant, machinery or vehicles you think you need on a long-term basis. Is it not really a luxury to own something that could be hired? Could you save money by hiring instead of buying? Would it be wiser not to tie up your capital? Would you be more likely to make profits which you could wisely invest in your prosperous future? Remember that before you tie up your capital in fixed assets you must have secured your long-term success.

Some of your possible needs for fixed capital and working capital might be an office, a yard, transport, plant and equipment. Figure I illustrates a typical project cycle where much of your money is tied up during the first months as working capital.

Figure I. The way the working capital ties up money in a construction business during a typical project

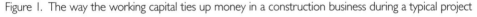
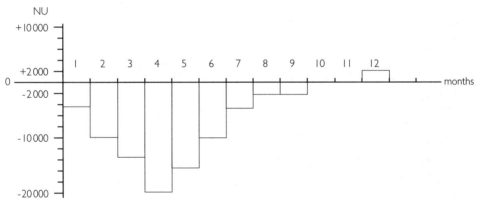

YOUR OFFICE AND YARD

If your business has been stable and profitable for a long time, you may decide to invest in your own yard. Consider carefully, however, whether you are ready to tie up your fixed assets in a yard, or whether you can afford to borrow the money from outside. If you can afford to borrow, decide if it is wise to do so. Interest rates tend to be high, and it may be difficult to sell your yard if you need the cash.

You may choose to rent a yard but to set up your own office with the necessary machines and equipment. Make careful calculations and forecasts before investing and remember that all investments of this type will increase your indirect costs for every job you get, which means that you will have to do more work and earn more from it before you make a real profit.

YOUR TRANSPORT

If it is possible to use hired vehicles or subcontractors for your transport needs, and if they are reliable and not too expensive, this may be the most cost-effective solution. If you prefer to buy a vehicle, consider first whether your business situation is good enough, since buying a vehicle means tying up some of your assets.

PLANT AND EQUIPMENT

It may be difficult to rent all the plant and equipment you need, which makes it necessary to own certain items that are needed regularly. But remember that although plant and equipment can save you money if they are productive and regularly used, they go on costing money in terms of depreciation and other costs whether they are used or not. Many tasks can be carried out either by labour or by equipment, so you may achieve lower costs by recruiting and training a skilled and motivated labour force. Think carefully about the type of work that you plan to undertake, and only buy equipment that is really essential (such as a concrete mixer for the builder or a roller for the road contractor). When you are considering buying other equipment, make a careful calculation on its likely productivity and whether it will really pay for itself. Remember that you rarely get a good price for second-hand equipment, so do not assume that you can get your money back by selling equipment if you find you do not really need it.

If a dealer offers you cheap equipment, ask yourself whether this is really a bargain. When you make decisions about what to buy, and how much to buy, consider the life span and quality of the plant and equipment. High-quality equipment often lasts longer and in the long run the more expensive investment may be more advantageous per year or per job. You must find out the alternatives in order to make sound decisions.

FINANCING PROJECTS

Depending on how much of your own capital is put into the project compared to the amount of outside capital, the financial costs of running the project varies greatly. In the construction business you have to wait quite a long time for payments, which means that the contractor has to finance the project until these payments are received. Costs are often particularly heavy at the beginning of a project (as illustrated in figure 1). If you have several projects, it would be ideal to schedule them so that when your ongoing job starts to bring in money, you start your next project and avoid borrowing from outside. However, this is often very difficult to achieve and you may be forced to use bank loans or other external finance to fund new projects. This type of working capital is expensive, and you must be aware well in advance of the need, the amount required and the costs in terms of interest and fees charged by the lender. You need all this information to price your projects correctly.

CASH-FLOW CONCEPTS 2

A cash flow shows all cash items received and paid out during a period, such as a week or a month or a year. Just as you cannot walk into a shop and buy something if you have no cash in your pocket, your business cannot hire labourers if there is no money to pay them at the end of the week. Remember that cash flow is not the same as profits. A cash-flow analysis is either a forecast, determining how much cash you will need at a certain time in the future, or a record of how much cash has been spent. It measures how much actual cash a business has or plans to need at any one time. When preparing a forecast you should always use your previously prepared records to ensure your forecasts are realistic. A business can operate without profit for a period of time but it cannot survive if it runs out of cash.

Cash flow in a business can be thought of as a basin with taps and a plughole. The basin starts with some water in it, in the form of the owner's capital. But water is always flowing out of the plughole as you pay out money in wages, fuel bills and so on. Money should also be flowing in through the taps in the form of payments from clients, or temporarily from bank loans or other sources. If the water level in the basin runs low, your business is in trouble. If the basin runs dry, your business is finished.

In a manufacturing business the cash-flow position often becomes reasonably stable, and only changes as overall demand rises or falls. In contracting the cash flow depends mostly on the progress of individual projects. This can be very difficult to forecast, particularly for a small firm that may have only one or two projects going at a time. For a small contractor with one project the cash flow might look like the following:

17

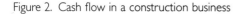

Figure 2. Cash flow in a construction business

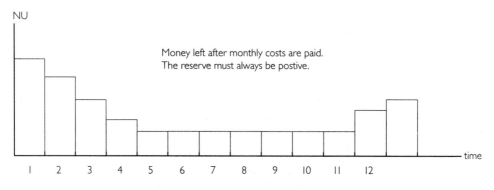

What you need to know

Cash flowing in: In most contracts you should be paid monthly for work done during the previous month. If your client pays promptly, your first payment should come in about six weeks after the contract commences. Then every month after that you should get a further payment. You may have signed a loan or overdraft agreement which helps you to get cash in when needed according to your cash-flow forecast. In some cases you may even have to sell property to help to get money in.

Cash flowing out: When you start work on a new contract you will first have to pay for setting up the site, providing tools and equipment, and buying materials. After the work has started you will be paying out all the time for wages and materials, interest, loan repayments and taxes.

Cash-flow analysis: Cash-flow analysis is a valuable tool. The cash-flow statement provides information about the way your business generates cash and uses it. Analysis of the statement is helpful in appraising past performance, showing why cash flow increased or decreased, in forecasting liquidity for the future, and in evaluating your ability to pay debt when due. It determines whether you are generating enough cash from your business to meet operating expenses.

Cash-flow forecast: The cash-flow forecast or budget prepared for cash planning and control sets out the planned inflow and outflow for a specified period. The cash budget helps the owner to keep the cash balance in the proper relationship to needs. It helps to avoid the two problems of idle cash and possible cash shortages. The cash budget shows how much cash

18

you started with (beginning cash), cash receipts, cash payments, and ending cash.

When you prepare a cash-flow analysis/forecast for the company as a whole, your projects are likely to be in different stages of completion. One project might be half completed, another just started, while a third is in the planning stage. To facilitate comparison between projects in different stages, the methods used for forecasting cash-flow costs and cash-flow income are designed to be compatible with calculations done during the construction stage.

The following chart (table 1) helps to explain the idea of cash flow and includes all the usual items needed for cash-flow analysis/cash-flow budget. The figures are not related to your project calculations. Work through them carefully if you are not familiar with the idea of cash flow. This will help you to understand the later chapters, and apply the cash-flow idea to your own business.

Table 1. The cash-flow budget

			January	February	March
RECEIPTS	1	Money present at start of month	200	700	2 600
	2	Cash sales	2 000	3 000	3 000
	3	Cash from credit sales	300	1 000	500
	4	Other money in	200	–	–
		Money in this month	2 700	4 700	6 100
PAYMENTS	5	Cash purchases	300	800	1 500
	6	Cash paid for credit purchases	500	300	2 000
	7	Wages	500	500	500
	8	Drawings	–	100	100
	9	Loan repayment	300	–	–
	10	Interest	100	100	100
	11	Others	200	–	200
	12	Planned investments	100	300	–
		Money out this month	2 000	2 100	4 400
		Money present at end of month	700	2 600	1 700

In the following chapters of this handbook we will show you how to calculate the project cash flow using receivables and outflows derived directly from your project. Then you can try calculating your cash-flow needs with the help of the workbook.

CASH-FLOW COSTS 3

Working capital is the fuel that drives your business. If you run out of it, the business will stop. If there is any danger of this you need to anticipate it well in advance, so that you can either borrow the amount needed, or reduce your expenses or level of trading to suit the funds available.

Before you can make a cash-flow analysis you have to forecast *costs* and *income*. In this chapter you will use your forecast of unit costs and your bar chart to estimate your total project costs. *Remember these are only forecasts of costs – you will have to check on actual costs and site productivity to make sure that they are realistic. If actual costs are higher than you forecast, you will have to adjust your future cash-flow forecasts and you may need to borrow money – as well as acting quickly to improve your business and site management.*

A project cash-flow analysis is a plan which shows how you expect cash to flow into a project and out of a project month by month over the whole project period. The difference between the two figures tells you how much you will have to put into that project in the early stages when costs are greater than income.

You need to know project expenditure well in advance, especially if a loan is going to be required to provide working capital. A typical construction project eats up a lot of money in the early stages unless a mobilization loan is available, and many construction businesses collapse simply because the owner runs out of money. Some of these businesses might eventually have shown a profit, but the owners could not find anyone to take the risk of lending to a business where debts were already overdue and the labour force were waiting for their wages. By forecasting your costs accurately and realistically, you can identify and deal with problems before they grow into crises.

To prepare a project cash-flow analysis you need to know:

❏ The direct project costs (from the estimate)

❏ The indirect project costs (from the estimate)

❏ The project income (from the quotation)

❏ The project time scale (from the bar chart)

❏ The method of payment (from the conditions of contract)

❏ The possible delays in payment (from experience).

Forecasting costs

A cash-flow *cost* forecast is the first step in preparing a full project cash-flow analysis. Costs can be forecast for the business as a whole, but in a construction business it is usually best to calculate them on a project-by-project basis.

Your project cash-flow *cost* forecast shows how much you will have to pay out to get the work done in accordance with the conditions of contract and when you will have to pay it.

❏ The estimated costs of the project were calculated in order to submit the quotation.

❏ The timetable for the work items is shown on the bar chart.

These two can now be combined to arrive at the project cash-flow cost forecast.

Note

The costs used here are taken from the total costs list also shown in Handbook 1 on page 73. The costs there are made up of direct project costs plus indirect project costs, including risk allowance.

A bar chart like the one in Handbook 2, pp. 20-21, should also be used to show when each activity is expected to take place and how long it will take.

TOTAL PROJECT CALCULATION

Item no.	Description	Direct project cost	Total project cost	Profit 8 % on direct cost	Total amount
1.	Clear site	30	37	2	39
2.	Excavate top soil	125	155	10	165
3.	Excavate foundations	375	465	30	495
4.	Steel reinforcement to foundations	863	1070	69	1139
5.	Formwork to foundations	284	352	23	375
6.	Concrete to foundations	477	591	38	629
7.	Steel reinforcement to columns	814	1009	65	1074
8.	Formwork to columns	572	709	46	755
9.	Concrete to columns	770	955	62	1017
10.	Concrete block walls to floor level	1565	1941	125	2066
11.	Return fill and ram excavated material, foundations	117	145	9	154
12.	Hardcore fill	727	901	58	959
13.	Mesh to floor	484	600	39	639
14.	Concrete to floor	1264	1567	101	1668
15.	Concrete block walls above floor level	1658	2056	133	2189
16.	Soffit forms to ring beam, openings	95	118	8	126
17.	Soffit forms to ring beam, infill panels	92	114	7	121
18.	Sideforms to ring beam	329	408	26	434
19.	Steel to ring beam	556	689	44	733
20.	Concrete to ring beam	669	830	54	884
21.	Fabricate roof trusses	1065	1321	85	1406
22.	Fix roof trusses	210	260	17	277
23.	Roof tile battens	184	228	15	243
24.	Tile roof	3138	3891	251	4142
25.	Timber to gable ends	215	267	17	284
26.	Form eaves	226	280	18	298
27.	Supply and fix ceiling boards	624	774	50	824
28.	Fix prefabricated window panels (including glazing)	1008	1250	81	1331
29.	Fix prefabricated door panels	354	439	28	467
30.	Terrazzo floor	442	548	35	583
31.	Bagwash walls and columns	249	309	20	329
32.	Paint	546	677	44	721
33.	External paths and parking	574	712	46	758
34.	Spread topsoil to landscape site	60	74	5	79
35.	Perimeter fence	418	518	33	551
36.	Dispose of surplus material off-site	129	160	10	170
		21308	26420	1704	28124

BAR CHART - CONSTRUCTION PHASE, AUGUST-DECEMBER

Item	Week no.	01	02	03	04	05	06	07	08	09	10	11	12	13	14	15	16	17	18	19	20
1-2.	Clear site + excavate top soil	▬																			
3.	Excavate foundations		▬▬																		
4.	Steel to foundations			▬▬																	
5.	Formwork to foundations			▬▬																	
6.	Concrete to foundations				▬																
7.	Steel to columns					▬▬															
8.	Formwork to columns						▬														
9.	Concrete to columns						▬														
10.	Block walls, up to floor							▬													
11.	Return fill and ram							▬													
12.	Hardcore fill							▬													
13.	Mesh to floor								▬												
14.	Concrete to floor									▬											
15.	Block walls, above floor									▬											
16-18.	Formwork to ring beam											▬									
19.	Steel to ring beam											▬									
20.	Concrete to ring beam												▬								
21.	Fabricate roof trusses								▬					▬							
22.	Fix roof trusses														▬						
23.	Roof tile battens														▬						
24.	Tile roof																▬				
25.	Timber to gable ends																▬				
26.	Form eaves																	▬			
27.	Ceiling boards													▬							
28-29.	Prefabricated panels																▬				
30.	Terrazzo floor																		▬		
31.	Bagwash walls and columns																		▬	▬	
32.	Paint																				▬
33.	Paths and parking												▬								
34.	Spread topsoil																		▬		
35.	Fence											▬		▬					▬		
36.	Surplus material off-site																				▬

CALCULATING CASH FLOW - COSTS PER ITEM PER WEEK *(rounded off to even number)*

Item no.	Description	Total project cost	Number of weeks	Cost per week
1-2.	Clear site, excavate top soil	192	1	192
3.	Excavate foundations	465	2.5	186
4.	Steel reinforcement to foundations	1070	2	535
5.	Formwork to foundations	352	2	176
6.	Concrete to foundations	591	1.5	394
7.	Steel reinforcement to columns	1009	2	504
8.	Formwork to columns	709	2	354
9.	Concrete to columns	955	2	478
10.	Concrete block walls to floor level	1941	2	970
11.	Return fill and ram excavated material, foundations	145	1.5	97
12.	Hardcore fill	901	2	450
13.	Mesh to floor	600	1.5	400
14.	Concrete to floor	1567	2	784
15.	Concrete block walls above floor level	2056	2	1028
16-18.	Formwork to ring beam	640	2.5	256
19.	Steel to ring beam	689	2	344
20.	Concrete to ring beam	830	1	830
21.	Fabricate roof trusses	1321	3	440
22.	Fix roof trusses	260	1.5	173
23.	Roof tile battens	228	1	228
24.	Tile roof	3891	1.5	2594
25.	Timber to gable ends	267	1	267
26.	Form eaves	280	0.5	560
27.	Supply and fix ceiling boards	774	1	774
28-29.	Prefabricated panels	1689	1.5	1126
30.	Terrazzo floor	548	1.5	365
31.	Bagwash walls and columns	309	2	154
32.	Paint	677	1	677
33.	External paths and parking	712	1.5	475
34.	Spread topsoil to landscape site	74	1.5	49
35.	Perimeter fence	518	2	259
36.	Dispose of surplus material off-site	160	1	160
		26420		

Calculating the cash-flow costs for a project

The "cash flow – costs per item per week" chart shows how to arrive at a weekly cost per item of work on the project.

Columns one, two and three (Item no.; Description; Total project cost) contain information obtained from the "Total project cost" calculation, explained in detail in Handbook 1, Chapter 7.

Column four (Number of weeks) is taken from the bar chart, explained in detail in Handbook 2, Chapter 3.

Column five is the result of a simple calculation where you divide the total project cost by the number of weeks expected to take to complete the item (column three divided by column four).

Now that we know the weekly cost for each item that appears this month, the next step is to set up a table that will allow us to calculate the overall cost per month on this project. The calculation is really very simple.

First, we look at the bar chart and find out what activities are planned for the month (i.e. four weeks). Secondly, we note the number of weeks that each item occurs *in that month*. Thirdly, we multiply the number of weeks by the previously calculated cost per week and get the cost of the item for this month. It is always best to set out the calculation in the form of a table, so that it is easy to make – and easy to check (see table 2).

Table 2. Example of a cash flow: Costs per month

Month	Item no.	Number of weeks that the item appears in this month	Cost per item per week (NU)	Number of weeks x Cost per week = Cost of the item for this month (NU)	Total cost of all items appearing this month (NU)
First month	1-2	1	192	192	
	3	2.5	186	465	
	4	2	535	1 070	
	5	2	176	352	
	6	1	394	394	
	7	0.5	504	252	2 725

The above calculation has to be repeated for each month of the project. You will have a chance to try your skills at this in the workbook.

Each individual monthly total should be entered in another table as shown below in table 3. We have left room for more columns on the right of the table, so that it will be possible to put in the monthly income and calculate the monthly cash flow.

Table 3. Project cash-flow cost forecast

Month	Project cost	
August	2 725	
September	6 752	
October	6 243	
November	6 998	
December	3 699	
January		
February		
March		
April		
May		
June		
July		
Total	26 417	

Compare "Total" (26,417) with the "Total project cost" (26,420) in your "Cost per item per week" chart (page 25). They should, of course, be the same (the difference here comes from rounding off figures, to avoid using decimal points). Monthly costs are illustrated in the following diagram (see figure 3):

Figure 3. Monthly costs

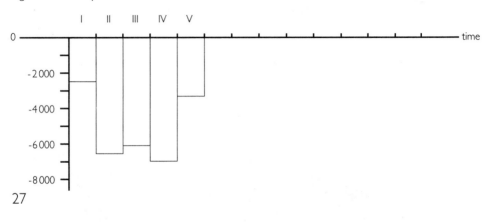

In Figure 1 on page 13 these costs are accumulated during the progress of the project and offset gradually by the income from payment of the claims.

Calculating your business cash-flow costs

By combining the relevant costs for the rest of your projects, you are ready to prepare the total calculation of your business cash flow. The more accurate and realistic your plan, the better the chances of your calculation proving correct. Remember that you should try to be *realistic rather than optimistic,* as in planning your project activities on the construction site. As stated in Chapter 2, your projects are likely to be at a different stage of completion so remember to use methods that will make the figures compatible, regardless of construction phase.

Cash-flow cost summary

Once you have prepared the cash-flow cost calculation for all your projects you will be able to combine them and get a clear picture of any likely shortages of cash and when these might occur. You will then be in control of your business; you can plan to defer payments or obtain money from clients more quickly so as to avoid running into a cash crisis.

CASH-FLOW INCOME 4

Income from measured work

Your contract includes an agreement on how you will send your bills to the consultant or client after you have started working. You have probably agreed about monthly measurement of work done and billing each month according to that amount. When preparing a cash-flow forecast it is useful to go through the same stages as when measuring work for the bill during the construction stage. It facilitates comparison and follow up later on and ensures that figures calculated for your entire company (i.e. several projects in different stages of completion) are compatible. In Chapter 6, you will learn more about measurement and the technical aspects of interim payments.

Adjustments for retention

From the measured amount you have to subtract a percentage for retention money. The retention money is kept by the client as a guarantee that the work will be properly completed. Part of the retention money is released when the contractor is entitled to a certificate of substantial completion, and the reminder at the end of the maintenance period. Some clients are very slow to release retention money, so you must make a realistic forecast of when that money will be paid into your bank account.

When will they pay?

It may be too optimistic to rely on the conditions of contract, which should stipulate the delay between reception of bill and payment. Your own experience is the best basis for deciding when to expect payment.

QUOTATION

Item no.	Description	Unit	Quantity	Rate	Amount
1.	Clear site				39
2.	Excavate top soil	m²	300	0.55	165
3.	Excavate foundations	m³	75	6.6	495
4.	Steel reinforcement to foundations 12 mm	lin.m	900		1 139
	8 mm		216		
5.	Formwork to foundations	m²	54	6.94	375
6.	Concrete to foundations	m³	12.0	52.42	629
7.	Steel reinforcement to columns 12 mm	lin.m	693		1074
	8 mm		228		
8.	Formwork to columns	m²	147	5.14	755
9.	Concrete to columns	m³	11.1	91.62	1017
10.	Concrete block walls to floor level	m²	96	21.52	2066
11.	Return fill and ram excavated material, foundations	m³	51	3.02	154
12.	Hardcore fill	m³	51	18.80	959
13.	Mesh to floor	m²	153	4.18	639
14.	Concrete to floor	m³	20.4	81.76	1668
15.	Concrete block walls above floor level	m²	102	21.46	2189
16.	Soffit forms to ring beam, openings	m²	9	14.00	126
17.	Soffit forms to ring beam, infill panel	m²	7	17.29	121
18.	Sideforms to ring beam	m²	54	8.04	434
19.	Steel to ring beam 12 mm	lin.m	432		733
	8 mm		162		
20.	Concrete to ring beam	m³	7.8	113.33	884
21.	Fabricate roof trusses	No.	33	42.61	1 406
22.	Fix roof trusses	No.	33	8.39	277
23.	Roof tile battens	lin.m	636	0.38	243
24.	Tile roof	m²	243	17.04	4 142
25.	Timber to gable ends	m²	18	15.78	284
26.	Form eaves	lin.m	108	2.76	298
27.	Supply and fix ceiling boards	m²	126	6.54	824
28.	Fix prefabricated window panels (including glazing)	No.	12	110.92	1 331
29.	Fix prefabricated door panels	No.	3	155.67	467
30.	Terrazzo floor	m²	132	4.42	583
31.	Bagwash walls and columns	m²	144	2.28	329
32.	Paint	m²	270	2.67	721
33.	External paths and parking	m²	146	5.19	758
34.	Spread topsoil to landscape site	m²	300	0.26	79
35.	Perimeter fence	lin.m	115	4.79	551
36.	Dispose of surplus material off-site	m³	65	2.62	170
	Tender bids to complete the works				28 124
	Plus 10 % for contingencies (if required)				2 812
	FINAL QUOTATION SUBMITTED				30 936

BAR CHART - CONSTRUCTION PHASE, AUGUST-DECEMBER

Item		Week no.	01	02	03	04	05	06	07	08	09	10	11	12	13	14	15	16	17	18	19	20
1-2.	Clear site + excavate top soil		■																			
3.	Excavate foundations			▬	▬																	
4.	Steel to foundations				▬	▬																
5.	Formwork to foundations					▬	▬															
6.	Concrete to foundations						▬															
7.	Steel to columns							▬														
8.	Formwork to columns							▬	▬													
9.	Concrete to columns							▬														
10.	Block walls, up to floor								▬	▬												
11.	Return fill and ram									▬												
12.	Hardcore fill									▬												
13.	Mesh to floor										▬											
14.	Concrete to floor											▬										
15.	Block walls, above floor										▬											
16-18.	Formwork to ring beam													▬								
19.	Steel to ring beam													▬								
20.	Concrete to ring beam														▬							
21.	Fabricate roof trusses									▬	▬				▬							
22.	Fix roof trusses															▬						
23.	Roof tile battens																▬					
24.	Tile roof																	▬				
25.	Timber to gable ends																		▬			
26.	Form eaves																			▬		
27.	Ceiling boards																	▬				
28-29.	Prefabricated panels																		▬			
30.	Terrazzo floor																			▬		
31.	Bagwash walls and columns																			▬	▬	
32.	Paint																					▬
33.	Paths and parking														▬							
34.	Spread topsoil																				▬	
35.	Fence												▬		▬						▬	
36.	Surplus material off-site																					▬

31

Cash-flow income analysis

An operational cash-flow *income* analysis is the second step in preparing a full cash-flow analysis. You need to know in advance what the monthly payment applications are going to be and if they will cover the costs sustained during that month.

❏ The prices per item of work have been submitted in the form of a quotation (although this is done in advance it will be prepared as a certificate measurement).

❏ The date when the items of work are to be done is shown on the bar chart.

❏ The conditions of contract will lay down the agreed method and times of application for payment.

❏ Your past experience with delays in settlement of certified payments will help you judge how long it will be until the cash is actually paid into your bank account.

These four can now be combined to arrive at the cash-flow income analysis. We will now prepare an income analysis based on the quotation, the bar chart and the conditions of contract previously prepared in Handbooks 1 and 2.

The "certificate measurement" chart (table 4) shows how to arrive at a monthly income figure for the project. To make it possible to compare the figures, they are prepared in the same way as the monthly measurements.

Columns A and B contain information taken from the quotation. However, to be able to fill in the "income per item" column (B) you will need to calculate how much of an activity you are planning to undertake during this month.

The total income per month is shown at the bottom of column B.

At the bottom of column C job undertaken during previous months and already claimed for is summarized.

Column D is work measured this month minus previously claimed, i.e. work done last month.

Column E shows the deductions that, according to the contract, are agreed will be made by the client.

Column F shows the *actual* amount of cash that will be due for work completed during the month of August.

Since Items 6 and 7 will not be completed during this month we need to determine what proportion has been done and calculate the corresponding income.

Table 4. Example 1: Certificate measurement for August (from bar chart)

A	B	C	D	E	F
Item no.	Income per item work done at end of month (quotation & bar chart) (NU)	Work done during previous months (previous certificates) (NU)	Work done during this month (B - C) (NU)	Deductions to be made (from conditions of contract) (NU)	Amount due this month (D - E) (NU)
1	39				
2	165				
3	495				
4	1 139				
5	375				
6	419			10 per cent retention	
7	268				
Totals	2 900	–	2 900	290	2 610

From the bar chart we can see:

Time needed to complete item 6	1.5 weeks
During month 1	1.0 weeks
Time needed to complete item 7	2.0 weeks
During month 1	0.5 weeks.

From the quotation we have:

Total amount item 6	629 NU
Total amount item 7	1,074 NU
Item 6 (1.0 weeks/1.5 weeks) × 629 NU =	419 NU
Item 7 (0.5 weeks/2.0 weeks) × 1,074 NU =	268 NU.

Just like when we prepared a certificate measurement during the construction phase, we now measure all the work that has been done to the end of September and deduct the work done (and claimed for) in August (table 5).

Items 12, 13, 15 and 21 are not completed at the end of this month so we need to determine what proportion has been done and calculate the corresponding income:

Item 12 (1.5 weeks/2.0 weeks) × 959 NU =	719 NU
Item 13 (0.5 weeks/1.5 weeks) × 639 NU =	213 NU
Item 15 (0.5 weeks/2.0 weeks) × 2,189 NU =	547 NU
Item 21 (1.5 weeks/3.0 weeks) × 1,406 NU =	703 NU.

Table 5. Example 2: Certificate measurement for September (from bar chart)

A	B	C	D	E	F
Item no.	Income per item work done at end of month (quotation & bar chart) (NU)	Work done during previous months (previous certificates) (NU)	Work done during this month (B - C) (NU)	Deductions to be made (from conditions of contract) (NU)	Amount due this month (D - E) (NU)
1	39				
2	165				
3	495				
4	1 139				
5	375				
6	629				
7	1 074				
8	755				
9	1 017				
10	2 066				
11	154				
12	719				
13	213				
15	547				
21	703				
Totals	10 090	2 900	7 190	719	6 471

Although these certificates relate to the work done during August and September, we know that a cash payment will not be received until some time later. When will that be? To answer this question, you need to read the conditions of contract and also use your own experience. Even if the conditions of contract require payment within 28 days of agreement of the certificate, you have to judge when the payment will actually be credited to your bank account. Some clients are always slow to pay, and there is no point in pretending to yourself that their habits are suddenly going to change.

In this case we will assume that although you should really receive payments in October and November, they will probably only be paid into the bank in November and December. We also assume that all subsequent payments will be received three months after the work was done.

You can test your skill in calculating project income again in the workbook. We can now go back to table 3, in the previous chapter and add a column for "project income" as shown below in table 6.

Note that we include the income in the month when we expect to have it credited to our bank account, even though the conditions of contract might say something different. It is always better to be realistic than to fool yourself that you will receive the payment on time. In our calculation we record the income items in our cash flow three months after the billing has been made.

Table 6. Project cash-flow income forecast

Month	Project cost	Project income	
August	2725	–	
September	6752	–	
October	6243	–	
November	6998	2610	
December	3699	6471	
January		5981	
February		6616	
March		3633	
April		–	
May		1406	
June		–	
July		1407	
Total	26417	28124	

The retention money is expected to be paid back in May and July, 50 per cent each month. It is always good to make a check of the total sum and compare it with the total sum on your quotation (28,124 compared with 28,124).

Figure 1 on page 13 shows how you use this income to cover costs and produce a small profit towards the end of the project.

Figure 4. Monthly incomes, presented as a histogram

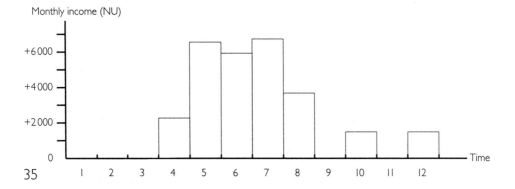

Business cash-flow income

To find out the total business cash-flow income, you have to make the same calculation of project cash-flow income for each of your projects. By simply adding and subtracting the columns for each project you get the total sum for each month. The process is the same as for the cash-flow cost calculations.

Remember that your income is more or less fixed after signing the contract. The only way to increase your company's income is by speeding up work on site so that more work can be undertaken. In contrast to income, costs are *not* fixed and they can easily rise unless you make sure they are carefully controlled.

CASH-FLOW ANALYSIS 5

The need for cash varies a great deal during the course of the project. In order to avoid trouble when the cash level is running low, you must know about such problems well in advance, so that you can either borrow the amount needed or reduce your activities. However, reducing the activities can be risky since your contract probably has a latest completion date that will then be more difficult to achieve.

You could think of the cash-flow analysis as the fuel gauge which tells you how much working capital is needed, by estimating future cash needs. A cash-flow analysis is a plan showing how you expect cash to flow into a project (income) and out of a project (cost) month by month over the project period. The difference between the two tells you how much you have to invest in the early stages when costs are greater than income. It also tells you how much surplus the project can be expected to yield later when income catches up with monthly costs, and hopefully overtakes them.

Calculating the net cash flow

To prepare a cash-flow analysis you need to know:
- ❏ The project costs (from the estimate)
- ❏ The project income (from the quotation)
- ❏ The project time-scale (from the bar chart)
- ❏ The method of payment (from the conditions of contract)
- ❏ The possible delays in payment (from experience).

We start with the table that we have already prepared showing monthly project cost and monthly project income. We will now develop this table further to provide a full cash-flow forecast for this project.

We can already see from table 7 that project income is going to lag three months behind the month in which the certificates

Table 7. Cash-flow forecast – Step I

Month	Project cost	Project income	
August	2 725	–	
September	6 752	–	
October	6 243	–	
November	6 998	2 610	
December	3 699	6 471	
January		5 981	
February		6 616	
March		3 633	
April		–	
May		1 406	
June		–	
July		1 407	
Total	26 417	28 124	

are prepared, that the first three months' costs are not covered at all and that the November cost is only partly covered.

After November, the certificate payments become more regular, with half of the 10 per cent retention being paid in May (it was actually due in January) and the other half in July, three months after the end of the three-month retention period.

Table 8 shows how these cash-flow cost and cash-flow income forecasts can be extended to make a cash-flow analysis chart, by comparing the project cost and project income figures, as for example:

August

Project cost	2,725
Project income	Nil
Cost higher than income	2,725

November

Project cost	6,998
Project income	2,610
Cost higher than income	4,388

December

Project income	6,471
Project cost	3,699
Income higher than cost	2,772

38

Table 8. Cash-flow forecast – Step 2

Month	Project cost	Project income	Cost higher than income	Income higher than cost	Net cash flow
August	2 725	–	2 725		– 2 725
September	6 752	–	6 752		– 9 477
October	6 243	–	6 243		– 15 720
November	6 998	2 610	4 388		– 20 108
December	3 699	6 471		2 772	– 17 336
January		5 981		5 981	– 11 355
February		6 616		6 616	– 4 739
March		3 633		3 633	– 1 106
April		–			
May		1 406		1 406	+ 300
June		–			
July		1 407		1 407	+ 1 707
Total	26 417	28 124			

January
    Project income   5,981
    Project cost   Nil
    Income higher than cost   5,981

Net cash flow is presented as a diagram in figure 5.

Figure 5. Net cash flow

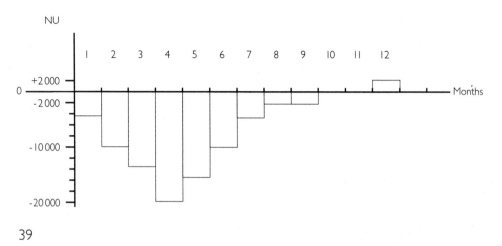

What does this tell you?

By extension of the chart (see table 8), a simple "cash-flow analysis" is obtained. The columns "Cost higher than income" and "Income higher than cost" can be filled in by simple subtraction.

The final column – "Net cash flow" can now be filled in, and both the contractor and the bank manager can see at a glance:

❑ The amount of cash input required

❑ When it is required

❑ The amount of income generated

❑ When it becomes available as cash

❑ The amount of money that can be repaid

❑ When it can be repaid.

The bank manager will want to see the calculations you have made when preparing the cash-flow analysis, so all submissions should be presented neatly and clearly.

Make it easy for your client

It is no good striving to find work, if, when it is done, the client does not pay up in good time. Most small construction firms are short of capital. If the client delays payment, money has to be borrowed (and interest has to be paid on it) to cover the cost of wages and materials.

It is the responsibility of the contractor to prepare the application for payment (commonly referred to as the "certificate"). After that, the client's professional adviser checks that it is correct and "certifies" that payment is due. Then the client should make the payment within the time period stipulated in the contract. The latter two stages always take time, but you can speed them up by making your application for payment easy to check. This means preparing it neatly and clearly. Like other administrative aspects of the contracting business, the preparation of applications for payment is not difficult providing you take it step by step.

Do it yourself

Some contractors employ professionals such as quantity surveyors or accountants to do this, but their services can be quite expensive. In this section of the handbook we show you how to prepare an application for payment or invoice without professional assistance. Then you can try out your own skills in the workbook.

To prepare an application for payment, measurement must be made of the work completed to date. Since the actual amount of work done on site often varies from that shown by the drawings at the tender stage, physical measurements should be made on the job. These should be checked and agreed by the consultant before the application is prepared and submitted for payment.

Some definitions

The *interim certificate* is a form which sets down the amount to be paid to the contractor by the client for the work done during a specific period, usually one month. The certified amount is the result of subtracting the retention money from the valuation.

The *certificate of practical completion* is issued at the end of the construction phase to certify that the work has been completed. Once issued, the client pays the contractor a part (usually half) of the retention money. The defects liability period then commences.

The *final certificate* issued when the defects liability period ends sets down the amount outstanding (including retention money). It is prepared after the final account has been agreed and any defects have been rectified. The remainder of the retention money should be released when the final certificate is issued.

Short-term work

BILLING YOUR CLIENT FOR WORK DONE

Get your bill off to the client as soon as the work is finished. If your business is big enough, it is worth getting a printer to print a book of sales invoices with your firm's name at the top. Otherwise you can type out the bill on the firm's headed notepaper.

In either case, the invoices or bills should be numbered serially so that it will be easy to check when it is paid or issue a prompt reminder if there is any delay in payment.

It is best to make out invoices in triplicate:

❏ The top copy is sent to the client

❏ The second copy is filed

❏ The third copy is put in a special file (or basket) of unpaid invoices, so that it is easy to check on outstanding debts. If you get invoices printed, you could have three different colours for the copies, so that they will be easier to sort out.

QUOTED JOBS

For quoted jobs, you can send the bill off immediately the work is finished, since the price was agreed before the job started. Thus:

> To painting of offices at Bonzo Stores, Malindi Street,
> as per our accepted estimate of 20 August . . . . . . 500.00 NU

QUOTED JOBS WITH EXTRAS

Where extra work is ordered after the original estimate has been accepted, it is always wise to agree on a price for that extra work before it is started.

Where this is not possible, you will have to work out the cost and give details of the extra work on your bill. In such a case you should always explain the reason for the extra charge in a covering letter. You might set out your bill like this:

> To painting of offices at Bonzo Stores,
> Malindi Street, as per our accepted
> estimate of 20 August. . . . . 500.00 NU
>
> To burning off old paint,
> preparing and painting three
> coats on the shop front . . . . 40.00 NU
>
> To cutting out and reglazing
> one glass pane. . . . . 20.00 NU
> _____
> Total amount due . . . . 560.00 NU

Stage payments

Stage payments are an alternative to monthly payments, and this system is often used for small jobs when it does not seem worth measuring the work done every month. These are payments made on completion of exact stages of a job.

For example, the stage claims put in during the building of a simple warehouse might be:

- ❏ Stage one – to finished floor level
- ❏ Stage two – to eaves level
- ❏ Stage three – to roof level
- ❏ Stage four – final completion.

Stage claims are also common on small materials supply contracts, for example:

- ❏ Stage one – door and window frames
- ❏ Stage two – doors
- ❏ Stage three – built-in furniture
- ❏ Stage four – final finishing.

Regular presentation of applications

On most contracts, applications for payment are presented at regular intervals, usually one month, for the duration of the contract.

Measurement

The amount of work done in the month is physically measured on site and the units are calculated and presented in the same form as the quotation. The procedure to follow is shown in examples A and B, covering work planned for August and September on our project. To make this example (example A) simple, we assume that the measurement complies with the quotation and the bar chart prepared for planning purposes:

Item 1:	Clear site	39 NU
Item 2:	Excavate top soil, $300m^2 \times 0.55$ NU/m^2	165 NU
Item 3:	Excavate foundations, $500m \times 0.5m \times 0.3m \times 6.6$ NU/m^3	495 NU
Item 4:	Steel to foundations (900m + 216m)	1,139 NU
Item 5:	Formwork to foundations, $54m^2 \times 6.94$ NU/m^2	375 NU
Item 6:	Concrete to foundations, $8m^3 \times 52.42$ NU/m^3	419 NU
Item 7:	Steel to columns (173m + 57m)	268 NU

It is always good to present your application for payment in a structured way that makes it look more reliable. Example A covering the month of August is shown below in table 9.

Table 9. Example A: August

Item no.	Description		Unit	Quantity	Rate	Amount (NU)
1	Clear site		m^2	25		39
2	Excavate top soil		m^3	300	0.55	165
3	Excavate foundations		m^3	75	6.60	495
4	Steel to foundations	12 mm	lin.m	900		1139
		8 mm		216		
5	Formwork to foundations		m^2	54	6.94	375
6	Concrete to foundations		m^3	8	52.42	419
7	Steel to columns	12 mm	lin.m	173		268
		8 mm		57		
	Total					2900
	Total: Measured work this month					2900
	Less 10 % retention					−290
	Measured work claim this month					2610

Extras

Work done over and above that tendered for must be agreed in advance by the consultant, who should issue a variation order describing the extra work to be done and the additional amount to be paid. Always make sure you have a *signed* variation order before carrying out extra work. Here are two examples of typical variation orders for this kind of situation, from example A:

Additional excavation to strip footings
due to bad ground conditions
(Variation Order No. 1)

Excavated volume: 10m x 0.5m x 1m = 5m^3
Rate from quotation: 5m^3 x 6.60 NU/m^3 = 33 NU

Total VO No. 1 = 33 NU

Breaking out concrete slab discovered just below ground level and not shown on drawing.
(Variation Order No. 2)

Breaking gang:
    4 labourers for 10 hours x 1 NU/hour =   40.00 NU
    Compressor for 10 hours x 2 NU/hour =   20.00 NU
    2 brakers for 10 hours x 1 NU/hour =   20.00 NU

Load and cart away rubble:
    1 tipper for 1 hour x 5 NU/hour =   5.00 NU
    1 f/e loader for 1 hour x 10 NU/hour =   10.00 NU

Supervision:
    1 chargehand for 10 hours x 2 NU/hour =   20.00 NU
    1 foreman for 1 hour x 4 NU/hour =   4.00 NU

Other items:
    Tipping fees: 1 NU/per load =   1.00 NU
    Purchasing of dust masks and safety glasses =   20.00 NU

Total VO No. 2 =   140.00 NU

Total extras claimed this month = 173 NU.

Materials on site

Depending upon the conditions of contract or quotation, contractors may claim a percentage of the cost of materials which have been delivered to site but not yet used in the job. The costs of these materials are usually claimed on the basis of the suppliers' invoices. Make sure that you keep these invoices and remember to include them in your regular applications for payment. In example A below, we will assume that the contractor only receives reimbursement of 75 per cent of the invoiced cost to allow for wastage:

Invoice no.	Description	Value (NU)	Less 25 per cent (NU)	Amount due (NU)
012695	Reinforcing steel	1 800	450	1 350
3962	Cement	800	200	600
Block-maker's letterhead	Blocks	2 400	600	1 800
Total				3 750

Fluctuations

Depending on the conditions of contract or quotation, you may be able to claim for national increases in wages or material prices. For example:

31 July   Government Statute No. 2369 – basic wage increased by 1.00 NU/day

14 August   Government Statute No. 2373 – cement price increased by 1.00 NU/bag.

Fluctuations claim for August (example A):

    8 labourers for 10 days × 1 NU/day = 80.00 NU

    12 labourers for 10 days × 1 NU/day = 120.00 NU

    Invoice No. 3962, dated 12 August:

    80 bags of cement × 1 NU/bag = 80.00 NU.

Total fluctuations claimed this month = 280.00 NU.

Interim certificate – Monthly valuation

(The following totals are brought forward from the calculation sheets on the preceding pages.)

Total measured work this month	2,900 NU
Materials on site this month	3,750 NU
Total application for payment this month	6,650 NU
Total extra work this month	173 NU
Fluctuations claimed this month	280 NU
Total	7,103 NU
Less 10 per cent retention	−710 NU
Total to be paid by client	*6,393 NU*

Worked example

Following on from example A on page 44, we will now work through example B.

Table 10. Example B: September (done at 1 October)

Item no.	Description		Unit	Quantity	Rate	Amount (NU)
1	Clear site		m²	25		39
2	Excavate top soil		m³	300	0.55	165
3	Excavate foundations		m³	75	6.60	495
4	Steel to foundations	12 mm	lin.m	900		1139
		8 mm		216		
5	Formwork to foundations		m²	54	6.94	375
6	Concrete to foundations		m³	12.0	52.42	629
7	Steel to columns	12 mm	lin.m	693		1074
		8 mm		228		
8	Formwork to columns		m²	147	5.14	756
9	Concrete to columns		m³	11.1	91.62	1017
10	Concrete block walls up to floor level		m²	96	21.52	2066
11	Return fill and ram excavated material		m³	51	3.02	154
12	Hardcore fill		m³	38.2	18.80	718
13	Mesh to floor		m²	51	4.18	213
15	Concrete block walls above floor level		m²	25.5	21.46	547
21	Fabricate roof trusses		No.	16.5	42.61	703
					Total	10090
Measured work, October = 10090						

EXTRAS

Variation Order No. 3

Additional concrete due to
extra excavation for strip footing.
(See Variation Order No. 1)

Extra volume of concrete: 10m x 0.5m x 1m = 5m³
Rate from quotation: 5m³ x 52.42 NU/m³ = 262 NU

Total VO No. 3 = 262 NU

Total extras claimed this month = 262 NU.

MATERIALS ON SITE

Invoice no.	Description	Value (NU)	Less 25 per cent (NU)	Amount due (NU)
3977	Cement	1 200	300	900
Total				900

FLUCTUATIONS

31 July   Government Statute No. 2369 – basic wage increased by 1.00 NU/day

14 August   Government Statute No. 2373 – cement price increased by 1.00 NU/bag.

Fluctuations claim for September:
     12 labourers for 20 days x 1 NU/day = 240.00 NU
     Invoice No. 3977, dated 18 September:
     120 bags of cement x 1 NU/bag = 120.00 NU.

Total fluctuations claimed this month = 360.00 NU.

INTERIM CERTIFICATE –
MONTHLY VALUATION

Total measured work 1 October	10,090 NU
Materials on site 1 October	900 NU
Totals	10,990 NU
Total measured work previous month(s)	2,900 NU
Materials on site previous month(s)	3,750 NU
Measured work + materials on site, net (10,990 – 2,900 – 3,750)	4,340 NU
Total extra work this month	262 NU
Fluctuations claimed this month	360 NU
Total	4,962 NU
Less 10 per cent retention	–496 NU
Total to be paid by client	*4,466 NU*

Make sure your clients know the terms

If you take on a contract subject to the standard conditions, then it will indicate how often payments along with your quotation should be made. If it is jobbing work, then you should state the terms of payment, to ensure you are familiar with the terminology. Take another look at the chapter on "specifications and conditions of contract" in Handbook 1, "Contract procedures".

SEND BILLS OUT PROMPTLY

Send your bill off *as soon as* the job is finished. The longer you delay sending your bills out, the less inclined your clients will be to pay them promptly. They are pleased (we hope) with the finished job and are more likely to pay up cheerfully as soon as it is finished, than some time later, when they have had time to spend the money on something else.

OFFER DISCOUNTS FOR PROMPT PAYMENT

This would only apply to jobbing work and the details of the scheme would be stated in your conditions of quotation.

You could offer a discount of 2 per cent for prompt payment (within 14 days of submission of the bill).

But if your profit margin is only about 5 per cent, then a discount of 2 per cent will make a big hole in your profits. So, if you intend to offer discounts, you should increase the amount allowed in your bill for profit to compensate.

MAKE SURE THE BILLS FOR JOBBING WORK ARE SUFFICIENTLY DETAILED

Make sure that your invoices or your original quotations give exact details of what the customer is paying for. Do not give the client an excuse to delay payment by disputing the bill.

Look at these invoices:

Description	Total (NU)
Repairs to house including tax	1195

Description	
Remove cast-iron gutters and drainpipe; replace with PVC Remove 2 panes of glass and replace Remove skirting board in living room and replace	Total (NU)
Materials:	
PVC gutters and pipe	325
2 panes of glass each 100cm x 600cm @ 118 NU	220
Wood 18cm x 1.5cm 21 metres @ 10 NU/m	210
Labour: 10 hours @ NU 40	400
	1155
Tax 10 per cent on labour	40
Total	1195

It is often a condition of contract or quotation that the client should pay an additional percentage as a penalty for late settlement of a certificate. While this is of some help in theory, in practice such a condition is very difficult to enforce. Unfortunately many clients do not take their responsibilities regarding payments as seriously as they should. The best way for a contractor to encourage prompt payment is to maintain good communication with the client, to ensure that certificates and claims are easy to check, and to avoid contracts with clients who have a bad reputation for delaying settlement.

Unless you are absolutely sure of a client's reputation, it is worth including an allowance in the estimate to cover the additional costs likely to be incurred due to late payment of accounts.

TRY TO AVOID LEGAL ACTION

The general rule is that the only people who gain from legal action are the lawyers, and if you take a customer to court:

❏ it costs you money, and

❏ you lose the goodwill of that customer, and get a bad reputation in the market.

WARNING LETTERS

Try sending out a series of warning letters, getting progressively tougher. You could start with a letter which is:

STRONG BUT POLITE

6 April 1996

Dear Mr. Simba,

In checking our ledgers we notice that your account for 4,000 NU has remained unpaid for over two months. We assume that this matter must have been overlooked, and will be grateful to have your cheque in full payment by return of post.

Yours sincerely,

George Ndugi

If that does not work, you can go on to send a letter which is:

TOUGH

20 April 1996

Dear Sir,

In spite of our letter of 6 April, there has been no cheque from you yet in settlement of your outstanding balance. Please send your cheque immediately upon receipt of this letter, and telephone me to confirm that it is in the post.

Yours faithfully,

George Ndugi

If that does not work, the next letter will have to be:

VERY TOUGH

---

4 May 1996

Sir,

In spite of two reminders, your outstanding balance still remains unpaid. Unless the amount is settled within seven days of the date on this letter, we will be obliged to initiate legal action for recovery of the debt.

Yours faithfully,

George Ndugi

COSTING PLANT AND
EQUIPMENT 7

Calculate and save

Plant is expensive and so is equipment. You should know how to calculate plant and equipment costs so as to save money. Before deciding whether to buy or hire plant and equipment, ask yourself two questions:

❑ What do I really need?

❑ What can I afford to buy?

Recovering costs

If you buy plant and equipment, you must get the best use out of it and recover the cost. When starting your business, you will probably limit your ownership of vehicles and plant to a small lorry/pick-up truck and a concrete mixer. Equipment will consist of wheelbarrows, shovels and small tools such as chisels, saws and screwdrivers. These may be bought for use on one particular contract, but more often they are used over and over again on different jobs.

Hire or buy?

Most contractors use some mechanical plant, which they either hire or buy. The following table (table 11) should help you to decide what to do in a particular case.

Table 11. Hire or buy? Checklist of points for consideration

Consideration	Is it better to hire?	Should I buy?
I cannot afford to buy	✓	
The item will only be used occasionally	✓	
The item will be used quite often		✓
It will be possible to hire it out when it is not in use		✓
An up-to-date model is needed	✓	
An older model would be O.K.		✓
Maintenance and repairs are complicated	✓	
Maintenance and repairs are easy		✓
A very skilled operator is needed	✓	
It is easy to operate		✓
Special equipment is needed to move it around	✓	

Before deciding to buy, it is a good idea first to work out probable running costs, and compare them with what it would cost to hire.

Your decision on whether to buy or hire a specific item of plant should be based on a balanced judgement in which all these considerations are thoroughly considered and weighed.

Plant operating costs

COST RECORDS

The cost of operating plant and vehicles has to be charged to the different jobs they are used on. This means keeping individual cost records for all major items of plant, and also separating out different cost headings. The cost headings should include:

❑ depreciation
❑ licences and insurance
❑ fuel and lubricating oil
❑ repairs, replacements and maintenance
❑ overheads
❑ profit.

All these points will be included when we calculate hourly operating costs for a pick-up on page 58. Two of these points, depreciation, and repairs, replacements and maintenance, might need some additional clarification before we start calculating.

DEPRECIATION

Depreciation is a way of representing the declining value of an asset as a series of annual expenses. At the end of the asset's life, the total of the annual expenses is equal to the asset's original cost. Let us use an example to illustrate the meaning of depreciation. You have bought a pick-up truck and will depreciate it in your bookkeeping, using what is known as the "straight line" method, i.e. that the rate of depreciation is constant over time. Thus:

Pick-up truck, cost new   10,000 NU
Expected life five years
Rest (residual) value at the end of the fifth year   500 NU
Depreciation 9,500/5   1,900 NU per year.

We are actually saying that:
At the end of year 1 it is worth 8,100 NU
At the end of year 2 it is worth 6,200 NU and
At the end of year 5 it is worth 500 NU.

If there were no inflation, you would be able to use this money to buy a new pick-up. In practice, inflation is quite significant in many countries, and businesses have to retain some of their profits in order to maintain the *real* value of assets. You also have to remember that the estimated life of an asset for depreciation purposes *is only* an estimate. If the asset is misused or not properly maintained, it will wear out more quickly. If you take care of it, the actual life may be extended well beyond its theoretical working life, and your profits will be boosted during these "bonus years". Since you do not have to set aside money for depreciation after the theoretical working life, that margin can be used to increase your profit without charging more.

REPAIRS, REPLACEMENTS AND
MAINTENANCE

These costs are difficult to estimate. With new plant and equipment little will be spent. Later on more will be spent. Take advice from suppliers or knowledgeable friends.

A simple method is to calculate these costs as a percentage of the yearly depreciation. In the case of our pick-up, we allow 20 per cent (a figure often used) of the 1,900 NU, i.e. 380 NU will be needed each year for repairs, replacements and maintenance.

HOURLY BASIC COST

For our pick-up the yearly costs are:

Depreciation	1,900 NU
Repairs, replacements and maintenance	380 NU
Licences and insurance	300 NU
Total	*2,580 NU*

The pick-up will not work every week. Estimated time off work may be:

Holiday periods	2 weeks
Annual breakdown time	2 weeks
Annual maintenance time	2 weeks
Total	*6 weeks*

So it will be working 52 − 6	46 weeks a year.
Based on a 40-hour week, that is 46 × 40	1,840 hours.
So the hourly cost is 2,580 NU/1,840	*1.41 NU.*

HOURLY OPERATING COSTS

The operating costs will include the driver, fuel, overheads and profit. For our pick-up, this might be:

Daily cost of driver	4.00 NU
Daily cost fuel and oil (from records)	12.00 NU
Which gives a total of	16.00 NU
So the hourly cost is: 16.00/8.00	2.00 NU

1.	Add the hourly machine cost	1.41 NU
	Gives	3.41 NU
2.	Add 10 per cent overheads (0.10 × 3.41)	0.34 NU
	Now totalling	3.75 NU
3.	Add 5 per cent profit (0.05 × 3.75)	0.19 NU
	Gives a total charge per hour of	3.94 NU

The hourly cost has to be charged against the jobs or contracts that the pick-up truck works on. Our pick-up will probably work on more than one job during the day, so it is convenient to have an hourly rate which includes the cost of driver and fuel. In the case of plant such as a concrete mixer which stays a long time on one job, it is easier to have a daily rate for the machine, and to charge for the operator and fuel separately.

USING A LOG BOOK AND
PLANT HIRE SHEETS

You should buy a log book for each item of mobile plant and each vehicle that you own (in some countries this is compulsory). The driver must be instructed to record the purpose, destination, route and time of each trip in the log book, so that the costs can be shared between the different jobs it is used on. Where the vehicle is on hire or has to be charged to a particular site, a plant hire sheet should be prepared as shown below. *Make sure the sheets are signed daily on behalf of the client, to avoid arguments when you submit your invoice.*

| Item of plant...................... No.............. |
| .... Hire rate......... |

Date of move	To job no.	Date of charge	Period charged	Amount
Date and the job that the item of plant was used on		Write the date up to which the client has been charged	Write the length of time charged for	Length of time × hire rate = amount charged

DEPRECIATION OF WORKSHOP PLANT

Depreciation of workshop plant can be costed like construction plant. The examples given below assume no residual value:

Drilling machine	1993	Turning lathe	1991
Price	10 000	Price	25 000
Depreciation per year	2 000	Depreciation per year	5 000
Value end of 1993	8 000	Value end of 1991	20 000
1994	6 000	1992	15 000
1995	4 000	1993	10 000
1996	2 000	1994	5 000

Bandsaw	1990	Milling machine	1991
Price	15 000	Price	25 000
Depreciation per year	3 000	Depreciation per year	5 000
Value end of 1990	12 000	Value end of 1991	20 000
1991	9 000	1992	15 000
1992	6 000	1993	10 000
1993	3 000	1994	5 000

PREVENTIVE MAINTENANCE

Maintenance is necessary:

- ❑ to make sure the machine is always in good working order when it is needed;
- ❑ to make the machine last longer; and
- ❑ to spot wear and mechanical problems *before* the machine breaks down, so you can repair it or replace worn parts without delaying the work or losing hire revenue.

Ask the supplier what maintenance should be carried out daily and weekly. Then make a driver or operator responsible for regular maintenance, cleaning and prompt reporting of defects.

Spare parts are expensive. Unless records are kept, small items may be taken for unauthorized purposes and be out of stock when you really need them. It is best to hold spare parts in a central store, and issue them to the various jobs using a stores transfer voucher. The foreman in charge of the job should sign for them, and be responsible for explaining why they are needed.

MATERIALS PURCHASING AND CONTROL 8

Controlling stocks

It is vital to control your stocks of materials if working capital is short. Materials only start to pay for themselves at the time they are incorporated in the structure. Until then, they take up space in the store on the site, needing money to pay interest on loans, risking loss through pilferage and adding to their effective costs every time labour is employed in moving them from one place to another. Of course, it may well make sense to buy materials in advance if they are offered very cheaply or if some particular material, such as cement, is in short supply.

This chapter provides advice on how to save money on materials. On many contracts they represent the biggest cost item, and small savings through better purchasing or reduced double handling and wastage can make all the difference between profit and loss.

TYPES OF MATERIALS

Four main types of materials are used in construction projects:

Basic materials	bricks, sand, aggregate, cement, structural and reinforcement steel, pipes and drainage ware, construction timber, stone and precast units, roofing materials
Built-in components	windows, doors, frames, wash basins and sanitary ware, electrical components, heating appliances, timber fitments
Equipment	refrigerators, air conditioners, ovens and other electrical appliances
Finishing materials	bitumen, felt, glues, paints, varnishes, wallpapers, tiles, mosaics, cladding.

WASTE

One of the responsibilities of site management is the control and storage of construction materials. There is always some wastage of materials: indeed studies indicate that it is not unusual for wastage to amount to as much as 10 per cent of materials used. On some projects, materials can make up two-thirds of the total cost, so that wastage influences the profitability of a construction project significantly.

The main causes of wastage and loss are:

❑ faulty workmanship or bad quality control, resulting in demolition and rebuilding of substandard work

❑ setting-out errors due to human error or faulty instruments so that works are not to true line and level, resulting in demolition and rebuilding, or making up to true level

❑ orders not clear about quality, quantity or size

❑ excessive use of concrete (e.g. in bedding and haunching pipes)

❑ shallow rubble under slabs resulting in excessive making-up to level

❑ faulty concrete weighbatcher producing mixes that are too rich

❑ substandard materials, e.g. poor quality or faulty tolerances resulting in excessive rejects

❑ breakages, e.g. in loading, transit or offloading, faulty handling and incorrect methods of assembly

❑ faulty storage resulting in site or weather damage

❑ short deliveries

❑ wilful damage due to malice

❑ pilferage, theft and corruption

❑ substitution; e.g. using facing bricks on internal walls.

CHECKING UP

There are three ways to find out how much money you are losing because of damage and deterioration of materials:

❑ looking carefully around the site and checking through the site stores usually shows up examples of poor placing and storage of materials

❑ comparing figures given in orders, receipts and issues, and checking on remaining stocks

❑ measuring the work done and calculating the materials used.

62

PURCHASE ORDERS

Whenever materials are required, a written order should be given at least in duplicate. Blank order books can usually be purchased at a stationery shop. If your business is big enough, it may pay to have your own books printed with the layout that suits you best, for example:

Job no.	Entrepreneur's stamp or letterhead	Order no.

Purchase order to:
(From
materials
schedule)

Please supply the following goods:

Quantity	Description	Price
(From estimate and from materials schedule)		

Deliveries to be made as follows:

No earlier than:
(From
materials
schedule)

No later than:

Further instructions to deliver:

Signature	Name (printed)	Title

In order to keep site records, each project should be given a job number and purchase orders should be numbered serially. If you have a large number of projects, start the job number with a client code as in the following examples:

Project	Job no.
Culverts for Highways Department	HD/11
Clinic for Ministry of Health	MH/13
Side drains for Highways Department	HD/12
Car park for hospital, Ministry of Health	MH/14

Purchase order numbers can then be combined with job numbers for easy reference, for example:

HD/11/1	(Culverts, Order No. 1)
MH/13/4	(Clinic, Order No. 4)
HD/12/6	(Side drains, Order No. 6)
MH/14/3	(Car park, Order No. 3)

Remember that the purchase order is not just the basis for the legal contract between you and your supplier. It is also a vital part of your bookkeeping system.

When materials are received on site, the details should be entered *immediately* in a delivery book. The supplier should always provide a delivery note. Your foremen should be instructed *always* to check that the materials are exactly as described on the delivery note and that there are no breakages. This must be done *before* the note is signed. Any discrepancies should be noted in the delivery book and the supplier should be informed immediately.

Copies of delivery notes should be kept carefully so that they can be checked against invoices to provide evidence in case of any dispute. Much time can be wasted if delivery notes are lost, so make sure that your site staff get into the habit of filing delivery notes immediately after they are received.

The delivery book can be a hard-cover exercise book drawn up as shown on page 65.

Name of supplier	Delivery note no.	Actual date of delivery	Actual date of delivery compared to date given on purchase order			Is the order now complete?
			Early	Late	Correct	

The procedure for filling in the delivery book is:

At the time of delivery

❑ Fill in the first three columns.

Immediately after delivery

❑ Compare delivery date with date requested and fill in one of the three columns to show whether the order is early, late or correct. If the delivery is early or late, it might be useful to show the number of days that the actual delivery date differs from that requested

❑ Check whether the order is now complete.

This is an example of an entry in a delivery book:

Name of supplier	Delivery note no.	Actual date of delivery	Actual date of delivery compared to date given on purchase order			Is the order now complete?
			Early	Late	Correct	
Bill's Building Supply	14359	16 May 91	4 days			Yes
At the time of delivery			Immediately after delivery			

CHECKING ON WASTAGE

At the beginning of this chapter we said that the cost of materials in some projects accounts for two-thirds of the construction cost and that wastage often reaches 10 per cent of the cost of materials. Therefore, limiting wastage means increasing your profit considerably. A good way to check on wastage is to compare the quantity of materials delivered to site with the quantity used on the job. This should be done regularly. If your contract provides for monthly measurements, this check can become part of the measurement routine. Here is one way to do it.

Step 1. Check the quantity of materials delivered to site during the month from delivery notes:

Delivery note	Description	Quantity
01624	Steel	10 tonnes
32198	Doors	10 No.
62956	Ceiling boards	200 No.

Step 2. Check the quantity of materials used on the job to date from the application for payment:

Description	Amount
Steel	9 tonnes
Doors	8 No.
Ceiling boards	200 No.

Step 3. Subtract the quantity of materials used from the quantity delivered to work out approximately how much material should be on site:

Steel	10 tonnes delivered less 9 tonnes used	1 tonne
Doors	10 delivered less 8 used	2 doors
Ceiling boards	200 delivered less 200 used	Nil

A visual check will confirm any discrepancies, and the situation can be remedied before it goes any further. To be really successful in limiting wastage of material you must turn these checks into a routine which will help you to discover discrepancies at an early stage. You can take immediate action to correct the mistake. Less money lost on wastage = increased profit for you.

PART B
MANAGING YOUR BUSINESS

PREPARING AND READING ACCOUNTS — 9

Why you need bookkeeping

Bookkeeping for ordinary day-to-day transactions is basically the same for most types of business. The job of the bookkeeping system is to provide answers to questions asked by owners, bank managers or tax inspectors, who have a right to know what is going on. You need bookkeeping to keep track of how your business is doing and to forecast future costs, as well as to produce the annual financial statements for your firm.

What is bookkeeping?

This chapter describes the basics for setting up a simple and useful bookkeeping system. If you would like to go into more detail, you could obtain the general *Improve Your Business*, Handbook and Workbook,[1] or a specialist book such as *Accounting and bookkeeping for the small building contractor*.[2] Bookkeeping does not have to be complicated. What you need is a simple system which can be kept up to date, and which provides you with information quickly when you need it. It always pays to take time to think carefully about the system you need when you start your business, because many small businesses lose time and money through poor record-keeping and poor accounting.

The books used for keeping records are the ledger and subsidiary books. The ledger is the general book in which you enter almost all the figures arising from your business activities. The

---

[1] *Improve your business*, Handbook and Workbook (Geneva, ILO, 1986).
[2] Derek Miles: *Accounting and bookkeeping for the small building contractor* (London, Intermediate Technology Publications Ltd., 1978).

subsidiary books help you to remember important things such as invoices, purchases, wages, stock and so on. You may have a subsidiary book for each item. The number of subsidiary books you need depends on the size and type of your business.

The ledger

The ledger is the main book in which you enter almost all the figures arising from your business activities. It consists of a number of accounts. An account is a column which has a specific name; Cash, Bank, Sales and so on. For the ledger you must make two entries for each business transaction, *out* entry for outgoing items and *in* entry for incoming items. This is the principle of *double-entry bookkeeping.* Every item bought for the business has to be paid for. Every payment you receive is in return for some product or service provided:

Ledger					
Cash			Sales		
In	Out	Balance	In	Out	Balance

The rows and columns cross to make a series of boxes. The secret of bookkeeping is to make sure that the correct figures are written neatly in the correct box. When money comes into the business you fill the In box and when money goes out you fill the Out box of the Cash account. The third column is provided to record the balance.

Your purchase subsidiary book or "purchase journal" will contain the following information. You can buy an exercise book and make the columns yourself:

Date	Supplier	Invoice no.	Debt (NU)
9.4	Karibu Co.	1146	500
15.4	Timber Co.	2312	1 500
13.5	Tool Co.	5 829	300

Remember that in double-entry bookkeeping every transaction has two parts. One part comes into the business, the other part goes out of the business. For example, when you make a window frame in your carpentry workshop and sell it to a customer, the window frame ceases to be an asset belonging to the business and the money comes in. For this reason you have to make two entries for every business transaction:

In		Out	
Cash	100	Window frame	100

An account – What is it like?

In its simplest form, each account consists of a large T-shape. The title of the account is written in the bar of the T. Increases in the account are entered on the left of the vertical line. Decreases are entered on the right of the vertical line:

Title of account	
Increases in account	Decreases in account

Principle of double entry

Always remember the general rule that whenever an entry is made in one account, an equal and opposite entry must be made in another account. For example:

Materials account		Suppliers account	
Timber 100 NU			Timber 100 NU

Which accounts do you need?

Remember to take time to decide which accounts you need for your particular business. The ones you probably need are: cash account, sales account, raw materials account, capital account, bank account, wages account and equipment account. There is no point in having too many accounts or a system which is so complicated that you will never have time to make it work.

Keep it simple

As owner or manager you will have to prepare (or pay some-one else to prepare) financial statements such as the *balance sheet* and the *profit and loss account*. This can only be done if you have a proper bookkeeping system. If you are running a small construction business, your system of bookkeeping need not be so complicated that you have to hire a full-time accountant.

To keep reasonable financial control of your business you need records of:

❏ outgoing payments to suppliers

❏ incoming payments from clients

❏ the cost of each separate job

❏ loans and other liabilities.

If you have organized these records properly, you should be able to find answers to the following six main questions you are likely to confront in your business:

1. How much has the owner spent on the business?

2. What has it been spent on?

3. How much has been received from customers and clients?

4. What has this been spent on?

5. How much is owed to other people or firms?

6. How much is owed by others to the business?

On the following pages we will help you to set up a system for keeping these records, so that you can check how much money you are making (through the profit and loss account) and how much your business is worth (through the balance sheet).

WHAT YOU NEED

You need sufficient information to produce a balance sheet, a profit and loss account, and to enable you to trace back and explain individual transactions. The basic records you need are of three kinds:

❏ *Bank statements* Received monthly

❏ *Outgoing payments* Bills, receipts for cash and cheques, cheque book stubs, wage books

❏ *Incoming payments* Certificate payments, details of sale of materials, hire of plant, small job payments by cheque and cash.

WHAT YOUR ACCOUNTS CAN TELL YOU

You need to know three things:

❏ whether each job is making a profit or a loss

❏ the costs so far, both for the business as a whole and for separate jobs

❏ whether your clients are paying on time.

This information can be obtained without an accountant. If a balance sheet is kept up to date each month and details of all transactions entered as they happen, it will make the annual audit easier and the accountant's bill lower.

SOME BASIC RULES FOR
YOUR ACCOUNTING

❏ The business should always have a separate bank account - its accounts must never be mixed with your private money except when you put capital into the business or draw it out as salary or as a dividend on your capital.

❏ All business receipts, whether cheques or cash, should be paid into the bank as soon as possible – preferably on the day that they are received.

❏ All large payments should be made by cheque. Whenever you have to make payments in cash make sure you get a receipt on the spot. (Small items such as stamps or stationery will be paid out of petty cash.)

❏ Information can be obtained as follows:

Certificate payments	Cash flow analysis
Material costs and invoicing dates	Delivery book
Wages	Direct project costs, labour schedule and labour cost allowables
Plant hire costs	Direct project costs, plant and transport schedule
Transport costs	Plant and transport schedule and allowables
Company costs	Indirect project costs
Other costs	Indirect project costs
Other income	Cash flow/own experience.

76

THE PROFIT AND LOSS ACCOUNT
AND THE BALANCE SHEET 10

The profit and loss account is the scorecard which tells you how well your business is doing. Profit is the amount by which income exceeds expenditure; if expenditure is greater than income the net result is a loss.

The profit and loss account

The purpose of the profit and loss account is to show the level of profit, or loss, which has resulted from the firm's operations over an accounting period. This is done by listing all revenue income and then deducting all revenue costs, which have been matched to the accounting period. First we have to identify all revenue items. The following definitions should help:

❏ *Revenue income* would include all income that a firm earned in the accounting period. Normally this would be restricted to sales of goods or services to outside clients. It would not include such items as capital introduced, loans raised, grants received or income from the sale of assets.

❏ *Revenue costs* would include all the costs which a firm incurs as a result of undertaking its normal business activities; wages, raw materials, power, interest and rents.

Costs which provide a firm with something that will last over several accounting periods, such as a new vehicle or a concrete mixer, would be excluded (fixed assets such as these are subject to a charge for *depreciation* in which a proportion of the cost of the asset is written off during each year of its useful life - see Chapter 7). Repayment of loans would also be excluded.

The profit and loss account starts with sales and the value of work in progress, and deducts from that all the costs incurred during the period. The result is the gross profit. From gross profit we deduct all the remaining revenue costs incurred. A simple profit and loss account is shown in table 12.

Table 12. A simple profit and loss account

COMPANY KARIBU	
Profit and loss account for 1.1.1996 to 31.12.1996	
	NU
Sales	30 000
less *Cost of sales*:	
Purchase of raw materials	16 000
Gross profit	14 000
less *Expenses*:	
Rent	1 000
Insurance	700
Stationery	90
Delivery	80
Interest	2 500
Wages	3 500
Transport	1 200
	9 070
Net profit	4 930

Profit and loss accounts for large companies are much more complicated, and will include other items such as sales from investments, interest, taxes and dividends.

UNDERSTANDING THE IMPORTANCE OF THE COST FACTORS

You need to understand the cost factors in your business so that:

❑ you can submit realistic estimates

❑ you can compare your cost levels with those of your competitors and work out why your bids are accepted or not

❑ you can concentrate your efforts on clients and activities that are most likely to show a good profit

❑ you can avoid the kind of job that is likely to show a loss

❑ you will be aware of increases in unit costs, either as a result of general inflation or due to a loss of productivity on your sites.

GOOD ACCOUNTING INCREASES PROFIT

Accounting is a powerful tool. Learn to use it properly and you will increase the profit you earn from your business by:

❑ controlling your pricing

❑ checking your variable costs

❑ checking your fixed costs

❑ checking your financial costs

❑ comparing actual costs with the budget

❑ improving planning of future projects.

POOR ACCOUNTING CAUSES LOSS

If your accounting is not accurate and reliable, you will find out too late that your expected profit has disappeared. Were materials too expensive? Did your workers' productivity go down? You just will not know the answer, and you may never be able to find out. Remember that good planning and accurate follow-up are the keys to securing your company's profitability. If you fail to set up a good accounting system:

❑ it will be difficult to get a loan from your bank

❑ it will be difficult to get new projects

❑ you may be in trouble with the tax authorities

❑ your business may fail.

You do not have to wait until the end of the year to find out whether you have made a profit or a loss. Once you have set up a good accounting system, you can check your month-to-month situation with the aid of trial profit and loss accounts as well as with cash-flow accounts. If you do this, financial problems should never take you by surprise.

Preparing a trial profit/loss account

The following typical analysis sheets are for a contractor with two quite large long-term contracts plus various short-term jobs which help to even out the overall workload.

The two larger contracts currently under way are:

❑ Construction of a new junior school   Job No. ME/21
❑ Stores extension for Highways Department   Job No. HD/16

The accounts will be prepared to cover three months of trading, and are based on four assumptions:

❑ All blocks are made by the entrepreneur. Blocks surplus to the jobs are sold to other contractors. Cost code for block-making is BM

❑ Profits or losses at the end of each month are carried forward to the following month, in order to give a more accurate overall picture

❑ Assumed bank balance at the end of December is 100 NU

❑ Agreed bank overdraft of up to 5,000 NU.

Table 13. Analysis sheet for January

Date	Job	Details	Outgoings (NU)	Receipts (NU)
03.01	ME/21	September certificate No. 4		7 000
03.01	ME/21	Cash for wages	700	
03.01	BM	Received – sale of blocks – invoice 3216		200
07.01	Office	Car repairs – cash	100	
08.01	HD/16	Acme Building supplies – invoice 62319	2 200	
11.01	HD/16	Cash for wages	650	
13.01	Office	Truck license – receipt TD81942	150	
13.01	Office	Third party insurance – truck (no receipt)	500	
15.01	ME/21	Work by joiners for Taylor's office shelving – invoice 3217		2 500
16.01	HD/16	Cash sale of old mixer – receipt not numbered		600
17.01	ME/21	Cash for wages	650	
17.01	Office	Insurance for truck	500	
21.01	ME/21	Bill's Building Supplies – invoice 99221	3 700	
24.01	Office	Petty cash float	45	
24.01	HD/16	November certificate No. 2		2 500
30.01	HD/16	Paul's Plant Hire – invoice 66616	850	
31.01	HD/16	Cash for wages	650	
31.01	Office	Salary cheques	350	
			11 045	12 800

The surplus of income over outgoings is 1,755 NU.

So the bank balance should have increased from 100 NU to 1,855 NU.

Check these results against the figures supplied by the bank, to make sure the calculations are correct.

Table 14. Analysis sheet for February

Date	Job	Details	Outgoings (NU)	Receipts (NU)
03.02	ME/21	Cash for wages	800	
03.02	BM	Received – sale of blocks – invoice 3218		500
07.02	Office	Typewriter repairs – receipt 77226	100	
08.02	ME/21	Solid Cement Co. account – invoice 22321	2 500	
10.02	HD/16	Cash for wages	600	
14.02	Office	Company tax – receipt IRS 496	200	
15.02	HD/16	Hire of truck to Tom's Transport – invoice 3219		1 000
16.02	ME/21	Sale of surplus material for cash		800
17.02	ME/21	Cash for wages	700	
18.02	BM	Solomon's Sand account – invoice 97261	1 000	
20.02	HD/16	Bill's Building Supplies – invoice 99264	3 000	
22.02	Office	Petty cash float	50	
26.02	HD/16	December certificate No. 3		3 000
28.02	HD/16	Paul's Plant Hire – invoice 66638	600	
28.02	HD/16	Cash for wages	700	
28.02	Office	Salary cheques	350	
			10 600	5 300

The deficit of outgoings over income is 5,300 NU (10,600 – 5,300).

So the bank balance of 1,755 NU will be replaced with a deficit of 3,545 NU.

This means that the contractor has to make use of the agreed overdraft facilities of 5,000 NU arranged with the bank.

Table 15. Analysis sheet for March

Date	Job	Details	Outgoings (NU)	Receipts (NU)
05.03	ME/21	Cash for wages	600	
05.03	BM	Received – sale of blocks – invoice 3220		400
06.03	Office	Telephone bill – receipt GRO617	200	
07.03	ME/21	October certificate No. 5		10 000
09.03	HD/16	Acme Building Supplies – invoice 62375	3 000	
10.03	HD/16	Cash for wages	600	
12.03	Office	Tender documents – Rural clinic	100	
15.03	ME/21	Plumbing work – Repairs to boiler – cash		1 000
16.03	HD/16	Hiring of truck to Tom's Transport – invoice 3221		1 000
17.03	ME/21	Cash for wages	600	
21.03	ME/21	Bill's Building Supplies – invoice 99276	5 000	
24.03	Office	Petty cash float	100	
26.03	HD/16	January certificate No. 4		2 000
31.03	HD/16	Cash for wages	700	
31.03	Office	Salary cheques	350	
31.03	ME/21	November certificate No. 6		6 000
			11 250	20 400

The surplus of income over outgoings is 9,150 NU (20,400 – 11,250).

So the bank deficit of 3,545 NU will be replaced with a balance of 5,605 NU.

Earlier in this chapter the importance of keeping proper accounts was discussed. It was emphasized that it can be a powerful tool, helping you to increase profit by controlling pricing, checking costs, etc. In order to get a detailed picture, the profit or loss situation on individual jobs has to be calculated. The information relevant to each job can be taken from the company analysis sheet and put on a separate analysis sheet for each job. Costs attributed to "office" should be split between the jobs. In this case it is assumed that the jobs are of equal value, so the "office", or "company costs" can be split equally between them (see *Pricing and bidding* – Handbook). The incoming payments relevant to "block works" would also be treated separately.

Table 16 is an example of an analysis sheet for a single job.

Table 16.   Job No. ME/21: New junior school
(Analysis sheet for first quarter (Jan., Feb., Mar.))

Date	Job	Details	Outgoings (NU)	Receipts (NU)
03.01	ME/21	September certificate No. 4		7 000
03.01	ME/21	Cash for wages	700	
07.01	ME/21	50% of office cost	50	
13.01	ME/21	50% of office cost	325	
15.01	ME/21	Joiners, Taylor's office shelving		2 500
17.01	ME/21	Cash for wages	650	
17.01	ME/21	50% of office cost	250	
21.01	ME/21	Bill's Building Supplies	3 700	
24.01	ME/21	50% of office cost (approx)	20	
31.01	ME/21	50% of office costs	175	
03.02	ME/21	Cash for wages	800	
07.02	ME/21	50% of office cost	50	
08.02	ME/21	Solid Cement Co.	2 500	
14.02	ME/21	50% of office cost	100	
16.02	ME/21	Sale of surplus material		800
17.02	ME/21	Cash for wages	700	
22.02	ME/21	50% of office cost	25	
28.02	ME/21	50% of office cost	175	
05.03	ME/21	Cash for wages	600	
06.03	ME/21	50% of office cost	100	
07.03	ME/21	October certificate No. 5		10 000
12.03	ME/21	50% of office cost	50	
15.03	ME/21	Repairs to cannery boiler		1 000
17.03	ME/21	Cash for wages	600	
21.03	ME/21	Bill's Building Supply	5 000	
24.03	ME/21	50% of office cost	50	
31.03	ME/21	50% of office cost	175	
31.03	ME/21	November certificate No. 6		6 000
			16 795	27 300

Job profit for the first quarter for this first large contract is 10,505 NU, as can be seen by subtracting the outgoings from the receipts.

Table 17 overleaf is an analysis sheet for the second large job, the stores extension for the Highways Department.

Table 17. Job No. HD/16, Highways Department stores extension
          (Analysis sheet for first quarter (Jan., Feb., Mar.))

Date	Job	Details	Outgoings (NU)	Receipts (NU)
07.01	HD/16	50 % of office cost	50	
08.01	HD/16	Acme Building Supplies	2 200	
11.01	HD/16	Cash for wages	650	
13.01	HD/16	50 % of office cost	325	
16.01	HD/16	Sale of mixer		600
17.01	HD/16	50 % of office cost	250	
24.01	HD/16	50 % of office cost (approx)	25	
24.01	HD/16	November certificate No. 2		2 500
30.01	HD/16	Paul's Plant Hire	850	
31.01	HD/16	Cash for wages	650	
31.01	HD/16	50 % of office costs	175	
07.02	HD/16	50 % of office cost	50	
10.02	HD/16	Cash for wages	600	
14.02	HD/16	50 % of office cost	100	
15.02	HD/16	Hire of truck to Tom's transport		1 000
20.02	HD/16	Bill's Building Supplies	3 000	
22.02	HD/16	50 % of office cost	25	
26.02	HD/16	December certificate No. 3		3 000
28.02	HD/16	Paul's Plant Hire	600	
28.02	HD/16	Cash for wages	700	
28.02	HD/16	50 % of office cost	175	
06.03	HD/16	50 % of office cost	100	
09.03	HD/16	Acme Building Supplies	3 000	
10.03	HD/16	Cash for wages	600	
12.03	HD/16	50 % of office cost	50	
16.03	HD/16	Hiring of truck to Tom's transport		1 000
24.03	HD/16	50 % of office cost	50	
26.03	HD/16	January certificate No. 4		2 000
31.03	HD/16	Cash for wages	700	
31.03	HD/16	50 % of office cost	175	
			15 100	10 100

Job *loss* for first quarter is 5,000 NU.

On the analysis sheet for the Highways Department work (HD/16) we saw the importance of making a balance sheet for each individual project so that we can determine which project is making a profit and which is making a loss. Although the overall figures for the company might look promising and show a profit, individual projects might not be profitable.

This kind of analysis shows where you have to put in some extra effort, and helps you to sort out the problems and get each individual project on track.

Accounting is not a once-a-year job. If you assemble accurate information throughout the whole accounting year, then it will be easy to draw together the figures you have in your books at the end of that year. Remember that your annual accounts will only be accurate if they are made up of accurate figures.

Balance sheet

WHAT YOUR BALANCE SHEET
CAN TELL YOU

The balance sheet shows the financial status of a firm at a given moment, normally at the end of a trading year. It shows the *assets* the firm owns and the claims against those assets, or *liabilities*. A balance sheet must always balance, because what is left after debts to outsiders must belong to the owner or shareholders. If the two parts of the balance sheet are not equal, then an error or errors must have been made in recording the data or in calculation.

Both assets and liabilities can be *fixed* or *current*. In general *fixed assets* will not be sold in the near future, and *fixed liabilities* will be capital and long-term loans that will also stay in the business. *Current assets* include cash in the bank and work in progress which should soon lead to a payment in cash from the client. *Current liabilities* include purchases on credit, since the business will soon have to settle the suppliers' invoices and statement. Some typical assets and liabilities are:

Assets = What the business owns	Liabilities = What the business owes
❏ Cash	❏ Creditors (people to whom the business owes money)
❏ Bank account	❏ Loans (owed to the bank)
❏ Outstanding debts	❏ Owners' capital (owed to the owner)
❏ Equipment	❏ Retained profits (owed to the owner)

Table 18 is an example of a very basic balance sheet for Company Smith.

Table 18. A simple balance sheet

COMPANY SMITH Balance Sheet as 31.12.1996			
Owner's capital:	NU	Fixed assets:	NU
Issued capital	5 000	Equipment	3 160
Balance on profit		Office equipment	500
and loss account	2 750	Vehicle	1 940
	7 750		5 600
Current liabilities:	NU	Current assets:	NU
Creditors	2 200	Work in progress	2 400
Taxes	900	Debtors	1 300
		Bank account	1 550
	3 100		5 250
Total liabilities	10 850	Total assets	10 850

Your business image and your staff

Running a business is a full-time activity. But it is sensible to take a break from time to time to consider carefully what kind of company yours is at a particular moment, and what kind of company you would like to own. If there is a gap between these two, it means there is room for improvement. This is not unusual. There are few businesses which are perfect, so you should work out a plan which will allow you to apply the title of this book and *improve your construction business*.

There is a business review technique called a SWOT analysis, in which you look carefully at all aspects of your business and make a list of its *strengths, weaknesses, opportunities and threats*. You might find it worthwhile to make a list of this kind, and try to get a picture of your company as seen by your clients, your personnel, your suppliers or your bank manager. No doubt your company has some real strengths and opportunities, but do not neglect to list its weaknesses and the threats which it has to face. Perhaps the debts are too high. Perhaps it is short of work. Perhaps the vehicles and equipment are worn out and need replacement.

You should find out the true situation and then try to work out how to improve the resources available. Be honest and realistic. There is no point in trying to fool yourself. Work out a step-by-step plan for improvement. Do not try to solve all the problems at once; decide on priorities and then start to establish the new image through real action. You probably want others to think that your company is reliable and healthy, that it produces high quality work, and that it is the kind of business which will respond to future challenges.

Your own role is most important. How you work, how you behave and what you say all give an impression of your company and establish a pattern of behaviour for your staff. If you are honest and hard-working, you will attract staff with similar working habits. Take your staff into your confidence, trust them with information and make sure they know about your company's goals. When you recruit new personnel, remember to tell them the features you are proud of, and train them to represent your company in their dealings with others.

When staff perform well you should reward their increased output, not only with a bonus or salary increase but also by recognition, involvement and learning opportunities. Do not hire additional people if you could get along with those working at the moment by reorganizing the tasks. Your staff costs must be included in project pricing as indirect costs, which means that the more administration costs you have the less competitive you will be. If your employees are competent and willing to learn, teach them to be polite and positive when talking to customers over the telephone, when writing business letters and when negotiating. This will build up a positive picture of your company. In this chapter we will deal with some of these matters in more detail.

Contacts with customers

TELEPHONE

The following points are a guide to good telephone technique:

❑ Make sure that the telephone is answered promptly and politely. "Good morning, Betterwork Construction" is much more pleasant than just "Betterwork Construction", and simply saying "Hello" gives an outright negative impression.

❑ Some telephone operators answer by saying "Hold the line please" and forget about the caller. This is impolite and may lose business. Instruct your office staff to keep in touch with the caller and offer to call back if there will be a delay.

❑ Members of staff who have their own telephone extensions must be taught to answer the phone in the same way.

❑ Staff who are slow to answer the telephone, or do not return calls to customers quickly could also lose business for you.

Business letters

To produce good business letters, you must remember the following points:

- ❑ The first impression of a letter is important. Check the layout and presentation of your letters. Do they look good? Is the writing or typing neat? Is the letterhead neat and clean?

- ❑ Think about the purpose of each letter you write. Is it a letter asking for money, a letter ordering goods, a complaint about poor service or a letter asking for a loan? State your objective clearly and briefly.

- ❑ Begin your letter with the main idea that you want to put over and make sure that it is presented clearly.

- ❑ Present separate ideas in separate numbered paragraphs.

- ❑ Before you dictate a letter, write down all the relevant information. The easiest way to do this is to list the points you wish to make and build your paragraphs around these points.

Filing

You may think that the filing of documents and letters is just a boring administrative job, and that you have more important things to worry about. But the small amount of time spent setting up a good filing system will save a lot of time and effort in the long run. The job of a contractor is not just to build things. It is to provide an efficient service to clients and customers, and that means the business must control all the information required to run the project properly. Below are examples of the sort of information that you will need to be an efficient contractor.

WAGES

Information for calculating pay should include wage lists with the names of the workers together with their personal details, their total pay, deductions from pay and net pay received.

EXPENSES CLAIMS

Where employees travel at the expense of the firm, copies of the claims for expenses must be kept.

DATA FOR INVOICING

Information on each completed job must be kept, including details of labour and material and customers' orders.

COPIES OF YOUR OWN INVOICES

When invoices are prepared, two copies should be placed alphabetically in a file called "invoices outstanding". This is an essential file because it represents money which will come into your business when the customer pays. When payment is received from the customer, the two copies are stamped "paid". One copy is moved from the invoices outstanding file to the invoices paid file, which is also kept in alphabetical order. It is essential that the other copy of the same invoice is filed in number order, usually in a voucher file.

VOUCHERS

Good business practice is to use one general voucher file, in which all paid vouchers are stored. When money is paid or received, the relevant voucher is marked "paid", a number is written on it and it is filed in the voucher file in numerical order.

SUPPLIERS' INVOICES

These are invoices which you have received from suppliers of materials or services. They are usually filed alphabetically. Many small businesses maintain two files: "Unpaid invoices from suppliers"; and "Paid invoices". When the payment is made, a note is written on the unpaid invoice stating when and by whom payment was authorized and that the details have been checked. That invoice is then transferred to the file labelled "Suppliers invoices paid", again in alphabetical order by supplier's name.

TAX FILE

This file is for all tax matters relating to your business and employees.

LETTER FILES

Even in the smallest office there should be files for incoming letters and copies of replies. Letters can be filed alphabetically according to the client's name.

THE BUSINESS FILE

This file should be used to file the originals of all important documents relating to the business such as annual reports, board meetings, insurance policies and important contracts. The file with the original documents should be kept in a safe and the file with the copies can be kept with the other files.

OFFICE EQUIPMENT

Consider what kind of office machinery and equipment you really need, but keep in mind both efficiency and cost factors. In general it is best to start with simple equipment, and buy more sophisticated items when you are sure that they will pay for themselves in time saved or increased efficiency. Remember that money spent in your office can only be recovered by extra profitability on project sites. If you eventually decide that it is worth buying modern equipment such as computers, fax machines or copiers, you will have to make sure that your staff operate them properly and arrange for regular servicing.

COMPANY RECORDS   12

You cannot manage your business professionally without good records. To take one obvious example, most contractors feel they are sometimes entitled to make a claim for extra payment on a project or to permit an extension to the contract period. To have any hope of succeeding in such claims, you must keep clear records so that you can support your argument with facts. The first and most fundamental step in the preparation of successful claims is to have accurate and up-to-date records.

A second example is the need to borrow money. Your bank manager will certainly want to see your financial records before even considering a loan application. Thirdly, the tax authorities will be entitled to ask for your records in order to check your tax return.

Past records can also help with future plans. They allow you to make comparisons between different years and different projects, and find out what types of projects are the most profitable and whether your business performance is getting better or worse. They also allow you to prepare realistic budgets and estimates rather than "guesstimates".

List of company records

You will have to prepare your own list of company records to suit the particular needs of your business. You will probably have two types of records; those that cover the business as a whole and separate records for each of your main projects. If you undertake a lot of small jobs, you may also keep files on this work for each customer. You will have to work out a system that suits you; the boxes below contain checklists of some of the items you might wish to keep in your general business files and in your project files:

General business files

- ❑ Financial statements, balance sheets and profit and loss accounts
- ❑ Purchase orders
- ❑ Delivery book
- ❑ Records relating to purchase, repairs and maintenance of vehicles and plant
- ❑ Plant hire records
- ❑ Bank statements
- ❑ Copies of all letters
- ❑ Personnel records
- ❑ Safety records

Project files

- ❑ Sketch plan of the site
- ❑ Working drawings
- ❑ Specifications
- ❑ Signed contract
- ❑ Conditions of contract or quotation
- ❑ List or bill of quantities (and calculations)
- ❑ Direct project cost chart
- ❑ Indirect project cost chart
- ❑ Site instructions
- ❑ Variation orders
- ❑ Allowables
- ❑ Bar charts
- ❑ Labour schedules
- ❑ Plant and transport schedules
- ❑ Material schedules
- ❑ Daily records
- ❑ Site diary
- ❑ Wage sheets
- ❑ Cash flow analysis

You should store your records carefully and protect them against dangers such as fire or theft.

Losing your records could mean losing your business.

WORKSHOP MANAGEMENT 13

Many contractors have a workshop which they use to prepare joinery for their sites and perhaps also to make and sell items to outside customers. The workshop may also contain an area where concrete blocks are manufactured or a shed for repairing and servicing vehicles and equipment. If you have such a workshop it is really a separate business, which ought to pay its way rather than be subsidized by the profit earned on your sites. You may even find that running the workshop is more profitable and less risky than bidding for construction work. This chapter should help you to run your workshop more efficiently by cutting down on waste of labour time, raw materials, machines and working capital. It is written from the point of view of the manufacturer, but many of the lessons also apply to site work in the contracting business, such as bending steel reinforcing bars.

Contracting is basically a service industry, and the contractor is mainly involved in the *assembly* of materials, components and products. Running a workshop is mostly concerned with *manufacturing* the products and components that will be assembled on the construction site. The skills of *manufacturing management* that are needed to run a workshop are rather different from the skills of *construction management* that are required to run a construction site.

The main difference is that the manufacturer can establish a steady process and introduce gradual improvements, while the contractor knows that every job and every site will pose different problems.

This does not mean that manufacturing is necessarily any easier than construction. Many of the principles of good management apply to both types of business. Both require you to purchase and use resources (people, material, equipment and money) in a sensible and efficient way so as to provide a good service to your customers, and both require attention to marketing (the subject of the next and final chapter).

The principles of manufacturing are simple. *You start with:* inputs, which include raw materials (wood, steel, cement and so on) and parts (such as nails, screws and wire). *You use:* labour, equipment and services such as power which are available in your factory or workshop to manufacture products for your clients or customers.

Depending on your approach to marketing, these products may either be made to order (which means you do not have to carry expensive stocks of finished goods, but will have periods when work is slack) or made as standard items to be sold to casual customers (which means you can keep a steady pace of manufacturing, but you have to be sure that there will be a real demand for the items).

Many manufacturers produce both products to order and standard items, thereby achieving a good balance between steady incomes from standard production with the good reputation and higher profit margins you usually get when producing specialized products.

Six stages of manufacturing

To make it easier for you to find out where your problems are in manufacturing, it is helpful to divide the process into six stages:

Stage 1 – purchasing/storage

Materials and parts have to be bought at a competitive price. When they are delivered they should be checked and stored in a safe place until they are needed.

Stage 2 – processing

The materials are processed; for example, metal or timber may be processed by cutting, sawing, machining.

Stage 3 – assembly

The parts are put together to make a product or component, such as a window or door frame.

Stage 4 – finishing

Finishing stages include painting or polishing.

Stage 5 – inspection

The product must be checked to see that it has been made correctly and is ready to be delivered to the customer. Although final inspection is included in Stage 5, you should make sure that regular checks are made during the whole process of manufacture – this is also called *quality control*. It is said that *a good carpenter measures twice and cuts once.*

Stage 6 – packing

The product is packed in a suitable way so that it will reach the customer in good condition.

Not all products pass through all these stages. For example, reinforcing steel is stored and processed (cut and bent to shape), but not assembled or finished.

Cost cutting

Since manufacturing tasks are often repeated, you can save a lot of money through regular small improvements at each of the above stages. In the next section we help you to see where you can make major cuts in your costs.

CUTTING MATERIAL COSTS

Good buying

The cost of materials can be cut significantly by improved buying (stage 1). Even if you are satisfied with your regular supplier, it is sometimes worth getting alternative quotations to check that the prices are really competitive. But price is not everything. "Cheap" materials can turn out to be expensive if their quality is below standard and they have to be thrown away.

War on waste

Work that does not fulfil the requirements must be thrown away or sold off cheaply. When work is scrapped, you lose not only the cost of machine time but also the money which you would make if the product was sold. As a good manager, you should declare a "war on waste". Good training of workers, good tools and working conditions, good wages and strong supervision will help you to win that war by cutting down on spoiled work.

CUTTING LABOUR COSTS

This does not mean cutting wages. In fact it may mean increasing them by setting up a bonus scheme so that your workers can share the cost savings that they help to bring about. In most manufacturing operations, it is possible to cut unit labour costs by increasing productivity. This is another aspect of the war on waste - cutting down the amount of time wasted throughout the manufacturing process – but particularly during stages 2-4. Why is time wasted in the manufacturing process?

❑ because workers walk or carry materials through the workshop further than they need. This happens because machines, workplaces and stores are badly arranged (see "Workshop layout" below)

❑ because workplaces are untidy, difficult to work in and badly lit

❑ because tools are worn out, unsharpened or unsuitable for the job to be done.

WORKSHOP LAYOUT

Workshop layout is the way in which machines, work benches and storage in a workshop are placed in relation to each other.

Bad layout means that the product travels and is handled too much during manufacture, and that people have to walk about too much. With bad layout, the product goes back and forward between processes. This uses more labour and more trucks, leads to delays at machines and makes work in progress difficult to find. Space is wasted and the workers get in each other's way.

How much money are you wasting by paying your workers to walk unnecessary distances or carry things around? Management consultants make a good living by advising firms how to cut out these unnecessary tasks. You should try to think like a management consultant who is visiting your workshop for the first time. Make a drawing of the workshop, and think hard about how it could be replanned to save wasted movement and lost time.

Improving workshop layout saves most money in processes where the products or materials used are large and heavy, such as sheet metal working and woodworking. In joinery the savings from improved layout can be dramatic, because woodworking machines cut timber very fast. If the machines are located in the right order there is little delay between the stages of manufacturing. The time spent moving big and awkward pieces of wood from the store to the shop, round the shop and on to the machines may be five or ten times as long as the cutting time.

So, if you are in a trade where heavy materials are handled, think how you can cut the handling time.

You cannot always achieve the ideal layout, for example in an old factory building; but there is always one thing you *can* do.

Keep your workshop tidy!

Put everything in its right place so that it is easy to find.

Keep your gangways clear and tidy.

Tidiness saves time and reduces the danger of accidents – at little or no cost!

CUTTING THE COST OF WORKING CAPITAL

Most managers of manufacturing businesses say they need more cash. Cash enables you to buy raw materials, pay your workers and office staff, and meet all the other expenses such as rent, insurance, telephone and so on. In contracting, the rate at which your clients have to pay is normally set down in the conditions of contract. In manufacturing, you have more control over income because you normally receive your cash in two ways: quickly when you make cash sales and more slowly when you make sales on credit, since people sometimes take a long time to pay.

High speed cash

The faster you get your cash back after you spend it, the faster you make a profit and the faster your cash (working capital) increases. Therefore, the raw materials which you purchased should be processed and turned into finished goods as quickly as possible. Then they can be sold and the money from sales will flow back into your business.

It is very bad if your materials are held up for a long time in each section of your workshop. The more stock and materials lying in your workshop, the more working capital is tied up. You should try to organize your production in such a way that you manufacture with a minimum of materials and semi-finished goods held up in your workshop.

You can also reduce the money tied up in working capital by:

❑ delivering finished goods promptly to customers and getting payment in cash whenever possible

❑ making sure that the customers to whom you sell on credit pay in accordance with the credit terms (this means preparing clear and accurate statements, issuing them promptly and setting up a system for issuing reminders for overdue payments).

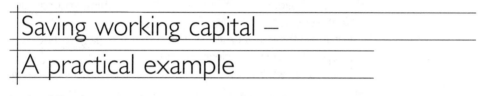

Saving working capital –
A practical example

In the following example, a contractor with a joinery workshop has been refused an additional loan by his bank manager, and has asked for your advice on how to generate more capital by reducing working capital. You take a careful look at his workshop, and calculate that the amount of money that he has tied up in work in progress is 48,000 NU. In order to explain his problem, you draw the following diagram.

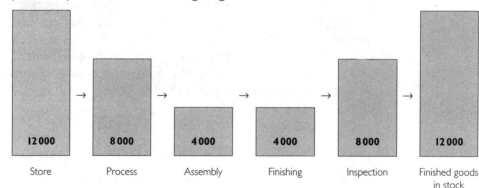

Store	Process	Assembly	Finishing	Inspection	Finished goods in stock
12 000	8 000	4 000	4 000	8 000	12 000

Most money is tied up in storage of raw materials and storage of finished goods, so this is where to start saving. You find that timber is often delivered three months before it is used, and the store is so full that carpenters often waste time trying to find the type and size that they need. By improving stock control and finding a more reliable supplier, it would be possible to order material two weeks before it is needed and the value of *raw materials in store could be reduced from 12,000 NU to 6,000 NU.*

Some frames are made in standard sizes for sale to casual customers. This is good business since sales are usually for cash, but you find that some frames are made in special sizes and there is only occasional demand for them. You suggest keeping only a few standard sizes in stock, but offering a special quick manufacturing service (at a premium price) for customers who need special frames urgently. This will mean a much quicker turnover of finished frames, and the value of *finished materials in stock can be reduced from 12,000 NU to 6,000 NU.*

You have now saved 12,000 NU on these two stages, but it is still worth looking at the other stages to see if more cash can be released. You notice that the workshop layout seems good and the employees work quite hard *when they have a job to do,* but there are two main problems:

❏ there are often gaps in assembly when carpenters are idle, waiting for processed timber to be brought by the labourers

❏ the inspection area is congested because the workshop foreman tends to leave inspection as a quiet job for the end of the week, and the carpenters often leave minor faults to see if they can "get away with them"

You suggest that the contractor should introduce a profit-related bonus scheme for his workshop employees (he already has one for his site workers). The result is that the carpenters and the labourers will have an incentive to keep materials moving through the workshop. It will be worthwhile to correct minor faults at the finishing stage and the foreman will also be anxious to maintain quality at every stage of manufacture rather than leaving it to the formal inspection.

Because work will be moving more quickly, you estimate that there will still be 4,000 NU at the assembly stage and 4,000 NU at the finishing stage, but *the process stage should be cut from 8,000 NU to 4,000 NU* and *the inspection stage should be cut from 8,000 NU to 2,000 NU.* The final result will be that work in progress will be *cut from 48,000 NU to 26,000 NU.*

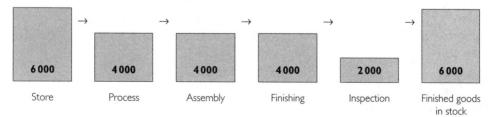

| 6 000 | 4 000 | 4 000 | 4 000 | 2 000 | 6 000 |
| Store | Process | Assembly | Finishing | Inspection | Finished goods in stock |

Remember

In the above example the money tied up in work in progress was reduced by moving materials and stock faster through the workshop. You can do this in your own business by starting the day with a "productivity hunt". Talk to your workers and ask their advice. It is almost certain that you will be able to make savings by:

❑ Improved workshop layout

❑ Improved workplace layout

❑ Better machine maintenance

❑ Quicker loading and unloading of machines

❑ Shorter machining time.

You can also reduce the money tied up by quick delivery of finished items to customers after you have sold the goods.

MARKETING 14

Why have we left marketing until the last chapter of the third handbook? Not because it is the least important topic, but because you need to understand and improve all aspects of your business in order to market your services or products effectively. Marketing is in fact the most important function of business, because a business without customers is no business at all.

Since you are a contractor, you are in business to offer a useful service: a capacity to build houses, roads, factories and so on. If you manufacture building materials, you are in business to offer useful products. Either way, if you do not have clients you do not have a future. But it is not enough to find clients. What you need are *profitable* clients, because clients who waste too much of your time or fail to settle their accounts are of no use to you or your business. A marketing plan will help you to earn a consistent profit, by offering the *right* service to the *right* people.

What is marketing?

Marketing is identifying and satisfying customers' needs at a profit. This means that you should analyse the needs of existing and potential clients, and also study your competitors' strengths and weaknesses, the products and services they offer and the prices they charge. Construction is a very competitive industry, and your competitors would be very happy to take your business away from you.

Remember: if you don't look after your customers,
someone else will

Your own role in marketing

Remember:

> There are those who make things happen.
>
> There are those to whom things happen.
>
> There are those who are looking on when things happen.
>
> There are those who don't even know what is happening.

You should take care that you belong to the first group. You should plan and decide what you want and make it happen. All construction enterprises face competitive conditions. Clients will not usually come to you. You have to seek them out, and persuade them that they will benefit from choosing you rather than one of your competitors.

Finding out what customers want

Business people must know their customers. Whether you are selling a service (such as contracting) or a product (such as building materials or components) you must find the right answers to many questions, including:

❑ *Whom* am I trying to sell to?

❑ *Where* are my clients or customers – in the capital city, in the provinces, in smaller towns or in the country?

❑ *When* do they buy – all the year round, in winter, in summer, at holiday times?

❑ *What* do they want, can they afford it and can I sell it?

Remember that your business could not exist without your customers. You need to understand their problems and priorities, so as to provide products and services that match their needs. This means that you should try to understand their business activities, as there may be opportunities for you to work together to your mutual advantage.

Finding out what competitors do

You should also take an interest in what your competitors are doing. You should never be too proud to learn from them, or to apply ideas which have helped to make them successful.

Promotion and advertising

Paid advertising is often expensive, but you may find it worthwhile to advertise in your local paper. Better still, you may get to know some of the reporters and be able to supply them with news items that provide free publicity. If you have just built a new shop or produced a new type of window frame, try to think how this could be linked to a news item.

For a construction business, it is normally best to target individual customers. The owners of businesses, bankers and top managers will read personal letters while they throw away a circular. Make sure your letters are on the best kind of paper with an impressive letterhead and check that they are very well typed. If your typist is not good enough to do this, use a typing agency. This is the way to promote a good image of your business.

Public relations

Every business needs friends. Public relations means communicating the image of a competent group of people who know the technical side of their business, and can be relied upon to give a good service to their clients without upsetting the general public. This need not be expensive. Make sure your sites are properly fenced to avoid danger to people passing by. Keep your vehicles and plant clean, and instruct your drivers to show care and consideration for other road users. Deal with complaints promptly and diplomatically. Make sure your site managers and staff are good ambassadors for your firm. Above all, make sure that your behaviour as owner/manager sets a good example of integrity and honest business practice.

What do we do well?

Very few businesses make the same profit on all their activities. Some make a good profit on providing some products and services, but lose most of it in other parts of their business. If you manufacture building materials as well as running a contracting business, you need to know that both activities are profitable. Even if you concentrate on contracting, you can split your business down into separate activities. For example, a contractor may make a good profit on house building, but lose money on roads and sewers. Guessing which activities are profitable is not good enough. You need to get your accounts into a form where you can check which types of contract, product or service make money, and also compare the profitability of various clients.

Marketing for contractors

Contractors have to decide what they can construct and where they are prepared to accept work. Some contractors will offer to build anything anywhere. This may sound a good policy when you are short of work, but it is bound to lead to problems. The secret of success for the small business is specialization – doing a few things really well in an area close to your base where you can supervise them closely to make sure that you satisfy your customer.

If you specialize, you stand a better chance of getting a name for quality. Most clients agree that there are many contractors, but few who can be relied upon to provide a quality job.

The two keys to marketing for contractors are: specialization and quality

Quality

Clients expect three things from their contractors: *quality* work, *timely* completion and low *cost*. Most small contractors face the same basic costs, so reduced tender prices usually mean reduced profits. Completion times for small projects are usually set by the client. This leaves *quality*. If you gain a good name for quality work, you will win contracts when others complain that no work is available.

Quality is not just good workmanship on the site, although that is an essential part of it. Quality is also about putting the customers' needs first. It means helping them to define their needs and then making sure that those needs are satisfied. It is an essential part of marketing just as it is an essential part of production. If you have a reputation for high quality, you will find it much easier to persuade clients and consultants to include your firm on tender lists. You may even be invited to negotiate for work, although you are not the lowest bidder. Quality means *taking care* in everything you do.

Marketing building materials

Building materials are products. They may be specified by architects or their clients, sold direct to contractors or sold through wholesalers or retailers. Whichever way your products are sold, they have to satisfy the ultimate user of the building. So most building materials and components have to be both *durable* and *attractive*. It is usually difficult to decide what will attract clients to buy your products. People like something a little different from what their friends have – but not too different! People change their ideas slowly and like things they know. If you make something too different, only a few people will buy it.

❑ Think about the product you are going to make and sell

❑ Try to imagine what the customers would like the product to be

❑ Remember that it pays to *specialize*. If you only make a few products, you can make them really well and improve your production techniques so as to manufacture them at low cost.

Distribution

Different products will be sold in different ways. The main decision for the small manufacturer of building materials is whether to sell direct from the workshop or to distribute the products through materials merchants. If you plan to sell products to public sector agencies or ministries, you will normally have to bid for supply contracts. Whichever way you choose, remember that distribution costs money and the cost of distribution must be built into the selling price. The main types of distribution cost are shown in the following table:

Method	Distribution costs
Direct sales	Employing sales and administrative staff or diverting staff from other tasks
Through merchants	Discounts
Tenders	Bidding costs

Discounts to merchants are the easiest to calculate, but the other costs can be even greater. The productivity of your workshop staff can be seriously reduced if they are frequently required to leave their main tasks to deal with clients. If you mix contracting with manufacturing, make sure that you have an accurate accounting system to divide the direct costs and overheads between the two activities.

Market research

Market research means finding out what your clients want, so that you can produce goods for which there is a real market. Products that fail to sell can eat up your capital very quickly, and you can save a lot of money by doing some basic research *before* you start to produce a new item. Market research need not be expensive. You can find out a lot about your existing and potential customers by:

❏ analysing your order book and sales records

❏ asking advice from your dealers and clients

❏ looking at manufacturers' catalogues and trade magazines

❏ consulting your local chamber of commerce.

Always remember to ask new customers how they first heard of your product or service. Besides showing them that you are really interested in keeping their custom, this will also give you with a good idea of how well your name is known and how your business is thought of in the market.

Sales records

Sales records are a mine of valuable information. From good sales records you can find out:

❏ whether your sales are rising, falling or about the same from month to month or year to year

❏ which products are selling well, which are selling badly, which sales are going up and which are going down

❏ in which areas the sales are best, worst or merely average

❏ which products customers like best

❏ which distribution channels are the most profitable

❏ how new products are selling

❏ whether older products are losing sales.

By having this information easily to hand you can match production with sales. If you see sales of certain products going down, you can switch production to other items which are selling better. Try to keep stocks of finished goods to the minimum level necessary to allow you to sell from stock. Remember that financing work in progress and storing finished goods both eat into your reserves of working capital, so time spent calculating your production targets as accurately as possible will be a big help in improving your cash flow.

Reasons for falling sales

Falling sales may be due to many different causes. Some of the most common are:

❏ one of your competitors is making a special drive for sales

❏ your products are not in line with new specifications

❏ your distribution channels are not working

❏ customers are unhappy with your quality (too many faulty goods), your deliveries (late, not in the right quantities) or your service.

Remember the benefits of *specialization* and *quality*. If you are known to be the best manufacturer of a small range of quality products, customers will always give you a chance to offer a quotation – and may even give you a chance to negotiate when they have been offered a cheaper price elsewhere.

Your marketing plan

Whether you have decided to concentrate on contracting or manufacturing, or to mix the two in order to have a more stable source of income, you need to bring together your separate marketing activities in a *marketing plan*.

The marketing plan will reconcile any differences and make sure that everyone concerned knows exactly what they have to do. The headings for a typical marketing plan are set out in the following table:

Heading	Notes
Present situation	Describe your business as it is today. The description will include the main activities, the resources involved, skilled staff employed, capital employed and profitability of all main activities.
Problems and opportunities	Identify likely changes in the market for your products or services.
Objectives	The description of what you intend to do should be set out clearly and quantified. This will include turnover and profit projections by activity and type of client.
Budget	The budget will take the objectives to the stage of preparing a projected profit and loss account and a cash-flow projection, in order to ensure that the objectives are within your firm's financial capacity.
Action	This should explain in detail *how* the objectives are to be achieved, *what* has to be done, *who* is responsible and *when* key activities have to be started and completed.
Resources	The plan will not be feasible unless the necessary resources and organization are in place. This section will spell out in physical terms the commitments that have been set out in the budget, and should enable you to check regularly on the progress of the marketing plan in the same way that you check regularly on the progress of your major contracts.

Producing a marketing plan for your business will take up quite a lot of time. Even so, you will find that it pays off by saving you from in a succession of crises when you are short of work one month and then take on more jobs than you can cope with. In Handbooks 1 and 2 we tried to show that *planning pays* on projects; this handbook has tried to show that *planning pays* for your business as a whole. The workbook will provide you with a chance to look carefully at your business, and work towards producing your own marketing plan to *improve your construction business.*